Ten Year Odyssey

TEN YEAR ODYSSEY

Margaret Wallace Conrad

www.ivyhousebooks.com

PUBLISHED BY IVY HOUSE PUBLISHING GROUP
5122 Bur Oak Circle, Raleigh, NC 27612
United States of America
919-782-0281
www.ivyhousebooks.com

ISBN: 1-57197-401-6
Library of Congress Control Number: 2003095716

Copyright © 2004 Margaret Wallace Conrad
All rights reserved, which includes the right to reproduce this book or
portions thereof in any form whatsoever except as
provided by the U.S. Copyright Law.

Printed in the United States of America

I dedicate this attempt to my two beautiful daughters, Sarah Maria and Micaela Kathleen. In the memory of a multitude of backpacking and camping trips, Caribbean cruises, and the "all in days" tour of Europe with them, I write this book. My wanderlust continued and was transmitted to them. Even though I had to go without them, I treasure those experiences we had together.

My thanks go to an author who forced me to sharpen five pencils, buy several legal pads, and start writing my story. One of his books, recounting his experiences abroad, was filled with references to endless drinking bouts, descriptions of brothels, the ugliness and discomfort he suffered while traveling, and biased appraisals of the inhabitants of the countries he visited. It was a sordid, pessimistic, and less than empathetic viewpoint. I was reminded of a quote. I do not know to whom I should give credit, but it sums up his perspective perfectly. "There are two kinds of men in this world . . . one who sees only the ugliness and the other who sees only the beauty."

I wanted to reveal a different traveling perspective, one of beauty.

Insatiable Lust For Travel—The Pursuit

Even though I lived two years in San Salvador, Bahia, Brazil and two years in Buenos Aires, Argentina, my story does not start there. This period from 1957-1962 has already been recorded in a book, which is being revised.

This narrative starts in July of 1983, when I took my elderly mother on an Alaskan Cruise on the French liner, *Rhapsody*.

The weather was rainy, but we struggled to enjoy every minute. We had a few difficulties, such as an outdated bathtub in our stateroom that resembled a fish tank. It was very deep and required a great deal of effort for me to help my mother step into it. She was heavy-set and arthritic. Otherwise, the accommodations were comfortable, the food marvelous, and the service excellent.

Most of the waiters were from Latin America. They put on miniskirts every night and sang songs that were hilarious in the Latin accent. These songs were old classics like "My Blue Heaven." That particular tune was done with the dance-song presentation resembling an Al Jolson routine. The thick Spanish accents produced a particularly humorous rendition filled with pathos that captured your heart. The waiters tried so hard and were really into it. It almost brought tears to my eyes. We were surrounded by gaiety, happiness, and a great desire to please. Even though I know the "dollar signs" of the *propinas* that were required were a great incentive, they still outdid themselves.

I became friends with one young waiter. I asked him where he was from. He said Tegucigalpa, Honduras. The name, Tegucigalpa, fascinated me. I made three trips there hoping we might meet again. It was an interesting city, where the planes slid in among the mountains to land. A huge neon Coca-Cola sign adorned the side of one mountain.

In spite of the cold drizzle, my mother and I made all the tours we could and wandered the wet decks.

We were taking the typical inland passage. After flying to Seattle, we boarded the ship and ambled up through the inside passage of British Columbia. Our first stop was Ketchikan. We came off the ship and went ashore to take a bus tour. They took us to the Totem Heritage Center, which held a collection of original totem poles. They were kept there after being retrieved from a deserted village. We wandered all around in the mist and on rain-sodden paths through villages and huts.

Coming back from our tour, we ate some salmon from the small outdoor charcoal grille set up where the passengers had to pass to board the ship. I have never tasted salmon like that again. I yearn for it . . . just one more time.

We walked on a boardwalk to get back on the ship. I was trying to help my mother when her foot caught on an uneven board. We both crashed. We got up again, making our way to the gangplank. There were no broken bones, only the desire to experience other vistas.

The next day, the ship edged its way up toward Glacier Bay National Park. Here was a myriad of shades of blues and whites. We saw the "calving glaciers" where parts fall from the face of the glaciers and crash into the sea, forming icebergs, which were floating about like islands. Glacial ice has exceptional density, causing it not to reflect other colors readily. Because of this, we were able to see the striking blue colors.

At one of our stops, we took a tour in a small boat, exploring southeast Alaska's bays and fjords. There were magnificent forests all along the shores. Many bald eagles were seen perched on the tall trees. We wandered in and out of many inlets.

The boat made a brief stop at Sitka. My mother was unable to go ashore. I dashed off by myself to see what I could of this unique town, founded by the Russian Aleksandr Baranov in 1799. He was a successful Russian trader and named the town Novo Arkhangelsk. After being destroyed by the Indians in 1802, the town was rebuilt and renamed Sitka. The strong Russian ambience is charming. The United States took possession of Alaska from Russia in 1867. Sitka was the capital of Alaska until 1900.

Back on the *Rhapsody* we sailed for Seattle to take our plane to Houston.

The Ship of Fools

In December of 1983, I could hardly wait to get going again. I wanted to escape the house, the family, the chores, the dog and the cat. Thinking back on this now, I was certainly shirking my responsibilities. I feel an annoying twinge of guilt, even after these many years.

I booked again on the *Rhapsody*, the French cruiser that had taken my mother and me to Alaska in July. Remembering the service, the food, and those handsome Latin waiters, I could hardly wait to get on board. First there was the flight from Houston to Miami. Everything seemed perfect. Then a series of events started to unfold.

The plan had been to sunbathe on deck to prepare for snorkeling tours in Puerto Plata in Santo Domingo and Puerto Rico. Tickets were purchased for fifty dollars. But, while sunshine is seldom lacking on the decks of the Caribbean cruisers, there came clouds, wind, and conditions not favorable for lounging. This went on for several days.

The ship arrived in the Dominican Republic amidst a great thunderstorm, which was a tourist attraction in itself. The tour director did not cancel the snorkeling. All who had signed up were kept waiting till late afternoon. The bus finally left with cheering snorkelers. It raced madly across a primitive tropical countryside. Upon arriving at the beach, everyone jumped out and raced toward the water, only to find huge waves crashing in. We all stood huddled together, listening to the instructor. No one cancelled, although it was obvious the conditions were impossible for snorkeling.

I joined five other experienced persons and headed for the buoy over the coral reef. It had taken native boys to help me into the water beyond the surf. When everyone finally gave up the struggle and started back, I followed. Near the shore, diving for a shell, I was picked up by a powerful wave and thrown violently onto the sand. My ribs crunched. A native boy helped me dress. Then back to the ship everybody went. The snorkeling expedition had been a disaster, especially for me.

The next port was the beautiful tropical island of Antigua. With my cracked ribs, I walked into the town taking photos, up one street and down another. I captured numerous picturesque people and panoramas.

The ship moved on to Puerto Rico where many other ships were docked. Bad weather cancelled all snorkeling trips and the money was refunded for the Dominican disaster also.

Here the steering mechanism went out on the boat and everyone was forced to sit in the harbor. The next scheduled stop in St. Martins was cancelled. By this time, all the passengers were getting disgruntled and threatening mutiny.

The ship was repaired and we were on our way to St. Thomas in the Virgin Islands. This was to be a scuba experience for me, but you cannot carry a tank with cracked ribs.

A madman, who was a passenger, had been harassing everyone on the ship for the whole trip. He was escorted off in St. Thomas. Three caskets carrying passengers who had died en route were removed as well.

At last, a bright light shown through. I was able to snorkel, following the ocean floor map off St. John's Island, even with the cracked ribs. I looked down on the coral reef, where the marine life was marked and named. I followed the arrows. This was an unusual experience.

Back on the boat, it was the night before New Year's Eve. The sea was very rough. As one danced, you would move "one-two" to one side then "one-two-three-four" to the other side as the ship lurched. This same evening after I ordered dinner, I realized I had forgotten my camera. I ran to my cabin, while the ship continued to rock violently. I dashed into the bathroom, camera on my arm, to put on lipstick. The ship swayed forcefully. Into the tile shower I flew. A gash on my arm required eight stitches before I could return to my steak.

There just had to be a turn of events, but on New Year's Eve the camera would not operate. All of the festivities and costumes were lost while I held my frozen camera.

The next morning, New Year's Day, as I entered the dining room for breakfast, the first words I uttered were: "It's 1985—right?" Just too much had happened for it to only be 1984. By this time it really didn't seem to matter anymore. I kept thinking that just to get back to Miami was all I really wanted!

The ship docked. It seemed like the trip had lasted several months. There on the dock stood the madman who had been removed in St. Thomas.

All of the passengers were milling around on the pier, looking for their luggage. I finally saw my one suitcase. It was like seeing an old friend. I raced toward it. Then I stopped suddenly. My eyes popped and my mouth dropped open. Here was a round hole in the side of my luggage the size of a pancake. Lingerie and other items were hanging out. I couldn't believe it. What a perfect ending to a complete disaster.

Jamaican Interludes

In May 1984, my sister called me from California to inform me that she and her husband, a dentist, were going to a meeting of dentists in Jamaica. I asked if I could go with them. I called my elderly mother to tell her the exciting news. She said: "I want to go too." Well, the four of us ended up in Jamaica. The name, Jamaica, comes from the Arawak Indian term *Xaymaca,* which means "land of wood and water." We stayed at a beautiful modern hotel in Montego Bay on the northwest coast.

Every morning as we tried to get down to breakfast, we were slowed down by my mother, who couldn't move that quickly, and by my sister, who was ill. She had a huge brace on her shoulder. My brother-in-law would announce in a loud cheerful voice: "Off we go like a herd of turtles." This was probably a very accurate description of the four of us moving slowly toward the outdoor eating area.

The buffet was loaded with all kinds of fruits and entrees. As we stuffed ourselves on the delicious variety of foods, many blackbirds landed on our table, hoping to share with us. They were very bold and showed no fear. They were everywhere, especially on the tables where the people had finished eating and had gone away. Not many of the crumbs were wasted.

Much like all the other tourists, we sunbathed by day and listened to reggae music and steel drums by night. This music was—and still is—different, appealing, and irresistible. The language, or local dialect with Ashanti words (Jamaican talk), is fascinating to hear.

One afternoon my brother-in-law and I decided to take the scuba test, which was required by the hotel before signing up for a scuba trip. You had to pass this test before you could go on a dive. All of the equipment was thrown into the deep end of the pool. You were expected to jump in and assemble everything under water. My brother-in-law, a very experienced scuba diver, failed the first time but passed the second time. He had been diving all over the world for years. I failed miserably and had to give up the idea of a dive. I did not have enough open water experience. So we went snorkeling together.

Another day we rented a car and drove along the north coast to Martha Brae River. We rafted this river with my mother and handicapped sister. We managed to get aboard somehow. There we were zooming down the river. A tall Jamaican with a long pole managed the raft and guided it by poking the pole into the riverbed. There were exciting moments.

We took another trip to Ocho Rios, Port Antonio, and the Blue Lagoon, also known as the Blue Hole. There was magnificent tropical scenery along the way, culminating with the breathtaking blue of this lagoon. On the way back, we rafted the Rio Grande. Again, this turned out to be an unforgettable experience with my disadvantaged mother and sister. We made it and headed back for our hotel in Montego Bay. It was getting dark and my brother-in-law had failed to buy gas. It was touch and go all the way back, wondering if we were going to run out of gas. My sister knew we wouldn't make it. My mother had no comment. My brother-in-law and I were optimistic. My optimism may have been a bit feigned, since I was trying to keep up his spirits. We arrived with all fingers crossed.

The next event was a bus trip to Negril. This turned out to be a spectacular jaunt. There were seven miles of pure white sand on the western end of the island. Bloody Bay, where the whalers used to carve up their catch, was very close by. We also saw beautiful cliffs and fine eaves. As typical tourists, we watched the sunset at Rick's Cafe. It seemed to be the thing to do, because there was an enormous crowd.

In July 1985, I took my second trip to Jamaica. I arrived in Ocho Rios, which is sixty-four miles east of Montego Bay. This town is situated on a bay sheltered by reefs and surrounded by coconut groves, sugar cane and fruit plantations.

A friend I had met on the first visit showed me around. We hired a taxi and took several trips. One was another visit to Port Antonio. Then we went quite a distance into the mountains to meet his family. The house was so remote that we had to leave the car and walk part of the way in. This was untouched virgin country, with many endemic fruit trees around the very modest houses. I saw the little house where my friend was born. His grandmother boiled some okra from their garden. It was superb. I have not tasted any okra like that since.

In August 1986, I returned to Ocho Rios. The third time should have been the charm. I was in a small hotel right on a private beach. After swimming, I would wander all around looking for a place to snorkel and for places to eat. I befriended many children who took me to meet their families.

A young British girl was staying at the hotel. One day we went sailing in the bay. Another day we made our way to St. Anne's Bay to rent horses. They were enormous polo horses. We rode up into the hills where there had been an old plantation and sugar mill, which was not operating at the time. We investigated all of the old buildings, including the ones that were involved in processing the cane.

I was happy to say goodbye to my horse. Next, I was to substitute him with a public bus. We left Ocho Rios, passed through the Blue Mountains, and dropped down into Kingston. I was neither impressed nor comfortable there, so I took a young girl out for a bite to eat and got back on the bus.

The bus was packed. I had to stand most of the way back to Ocho Rios. It took several hours. As we rattle-trapped along, I hung onto the ropes above, swaying back and forth. The mountainous countryside was beautiful, but I had to bend over to look out the window. The little hotel, clinging to the cliffs on the bay, looked so good to me.

Flashback

In June 1984, after seventeen years, I moved away from Houston. I came back to Arizona, where I was born. My elderly mother lived there in a small apartment. She invited me to stay with her for the three months it would take to build my house in Ahwatukee. This was a settlement in South Phoenix that was originally intended to be a retirement community. Later, the population growth got completely out of control. All kinds of people moved there, including criminals.

Being a science teacher, I started applying for a position in the high schools at once. One day, I had an appointment to be interviewed by the principal of a large high school in South Phoenix. The principal turned out to be a precious black woman. As I was getting ready to leave, my mother, who always wanted to go wherever I went, said, "I want to go with you." I said, "Okay."

On my arm, she hobbled along. We both went into the interview. I never thought how strange it must have looked, but I got the job as biology teacher.

Later, I found out this principal had an elderly mother who was not well. Eventually, she had to be put in a nursing home. To this day,

I believe that bringing my mother along for the interview influenced that dear principal, and had something to do with my getting the position. The memory of this incident makes me smile and cry at the same time.

I started hiking and camping with the Sierra Club and the Arizona Outdoor and Travel Club. There were numerous hikes in the Superstition Mountains, the mountains near Tucson, and Picacho Peak, located between Phoenix and Tucson. On one of these excursions, we went spelunking in a cave near Tucson. Loaded with two flashlights, lunch, and water, we had to crawl into the entrance on our stomachs. We climbed in and out of every nook and cranny we could find. It was different, but did not compare to the famous eaves like Carlsbad Caverns.

Spain, Portugal, and Morocco via Matzatlan

Since I was planning to go on a Cosmos Tour leaving from London in the summer of 1986 for Spain, Portugal, and Morocco, I took a modest spring break in 1986 to Matzatlan, Mexico.

Nothing spectacular happened on this trip. There was the typical inexpensive hotel very near the beach. Swimming and sunbathing took up much of the time.

There were long walks through the town, trying to find a restaurant where cabrito or chivito (young goat) was being served. Since living in Buenos Aires, I had an insatiable longing for this meat. In Argentina, it was a superbly succulent meal. The baby goat was halved and speared through with what looked like swords. The swords were placed upright all around an enormous charcoal pit. They were turned frequently, until the meat was cooked. I was not successful in Matzatlan. I am still pursuing this delicacy today.

Spain, Portugal, and Morocco

As the school year ended, I was getting ready to leave for London. This was the summer of 1986. Arriving in London, we discovered that our rooms at the inexpensive hotel were not ready for occupancy. This was bad news after having been on the plane all night. We sat around the lobby waiting. This wasn't much fun. Eventually, I did get to amble all over London by myself. As I had been there several times before, I did not go to the typical tourist's places. I stopped wherever something interesting was happening, as I strolled here and there. I looked for the fish markets on the streets and tasted all the different savory shellfish. I searched for an English metal teapot that so many hotel restaurants served tea in. I found one. I ran across parks and gardens and took numerous photos in Piccadilly. The next morning, we departed for the two-hour jet flight to Alicante, Spain, on the eastern coast. Again, everyone was free to explore this very small town. I walked along the ocean where a group of colorfully dressed girls were dancing. I treated myself to a beer and empanada. At dinner, everyone on the tour had the opportunity to get better acquainted. We sat around partaking of a huge platter of vegetables (menestra de verduras) and succulent pork chops.

The following day, the tour group boarded a large bus. This was to be our home and family for the next thirteen days. They say familiarity breeds contempt, but all of us were jovial. We enjoyed each sight, with the commentary, as we moved along.

We headed for Albacete, driving across the sun-drenched central plateau of Spain. Many wheat and barley fields, olive trees, and cork trees were sighted. We observed how they cut the bark of the cork trees, which is the cork. The cutting—how much and how often—is tightly controlled so that the tree won't be damaged.

We stopped for lunch in Albacete, where lunch consisted of "tapas." This is a large assortment of different foods resembling appetizers. I was given a piece of fish without charge. So I treated a little old man to a beer.

We continued, driving through Don Quijote's La Mancha. This is an extremely flat expanse all the way to Madrid. There were stops to photograph the famous windmills (molinos) of Cervantes.

Madrid is the capital city of Spain and is situated 2,180 feet above sea level. The Spaniards say it is the nearest thing to heaven. We were located on the ninth floor of a very large hotel, overlooking a Gypsy camp. What a contrast there was between the lavish hotel and the camp, which was made up of numerous shacks. They were built from an assortment of wood, cardboard tiles and other confiscated bits and pieces of material. In the center there was barren earth where the people gathered to mingle, wash their clothes in large pots, or use the crude toilet. I quickly made sketches of the unusual scene from my hotel window. For dinner I found a pub-like place that served blood sausage and octopus.

This next day was to be very busy with two organized tours—one of Madrid and the other of Toledo. Both consisted of the typical tourist's agenda. Both were very impressive and exceptionally beautiful. In Madrid, we went to the Puerta del Sol, the Rose Gardens, and the sumptuous Palacio, interspersed with shopping.

Puerta del Sol (Gate of the Sun) is the Eastern Gate of Madrid. It is the hub of the city, so to speak, from where all road distances in Spain are measured. Ten quaint and picturesque streets fan into its magical plaza. It is an intimate plaza, shaped like a half circle and lined with classical buildings.

Just off the Puerta del Sol is the Plaza Mayor, which is rimmed with old buildings and massive stone arcades. Bullfights were held there with thousands of spectators, many watching from the hundreds of balconies overlooking the plaza.

In the middle of the plaza stands an equestrian statue with a plaque summarizing some of its history:

> *Queen Isabel II at the Request*
> *of the Government of Madrid Ordered*
> *to Be Placed on this Site this Statue.*
> *King Felipe III*
> *Son of this Town, Who Returned the Court to*
> *It in 1606 and in 1619 Constructed this Plaza Mayor*
> *1848*

Historically, the plaza figured in the activities of the tragic King Carlos (1661-1700), known as El Hechizado (the Bewitched). He was the last of the Spanish Hapsburgs, with a severely handicapped body, and a mind that was probably on the brink of insanity. He was king from the age of three and, leaving no heirs, his death brought the Borbon rulers to the Spanish throne.

At the age of eighteen, King Carlos learned that many heretics were jailed in the countryside. They had been found guilty, but not yet tried nor burned. The king held a sumptuous auto-da-fé (Portuguese for act-of-faith) in this plaza. One hundred and twenty of the heretics would be brought forth for sentencing. This dramatic show took place on June 30, 1680 in the Plaza Mayor. On this day, fourteen hours were spent preaching to the heretics and reading their sentences, after which one hundred and one were dismissed with lesser sentences, like flogging, while the other nineteen were prepared to be burned at the stake. This was a grisly spectacle, organized by this sick king for his own enjoyment. Many of these performances took place all over Spain during the Spanish Inquisition.

The tour of Toledo was optional, but very rewarding. This old walled city on the Tagus was formerly the capital and Ecclesiastical center of Spain. The Moors came in 714 A.D. and took over. Alfonso VI won the city back in 1085.

The Gothic cathedral in Toledo was beautiful, filled with many paintings, a jewel room, and restored organs. High above were gorgeous windows displaying religious figures. Construction on the cathedral began in 1227. Today it is considered the finest cathedral in Spain. I could see the Mudejar style, which is Moorish, but built under Christian rule. Mudejar is the name given to the Moors who had converted to Christianity. The Mohammedan art achieved striking results. There are dominant geometrical designs which are oriental in the many embellishments created in the tile work, brick work, wood carving, and plaster carving. In one of the chapels, Mass is still celebrated according to the Mozarabic rite.

The Alcantara bridge built across the Tagus is of Moorish origin. The Alcazar palace built by the Moors has a fascinating history. During the Spanish Civil War, the insurgents, with their women and children, shut themselves in the palace after the Loyalist forces had taken the rest of the city. They resisted in July through September of 1936. They fought on the ruins until they were relieved on September 28th by Franco's forces. Only a fraction were still alive.

Toledo was made famous by the paintings of El Greco. Besides his paintings in the Cathedral, his famous "Burial of the Conde do Orgaz" is found in the Church of Santo Tomé. This city is like an open-air museum of Spanish art and history.

We left Madrid for Avila, the city of many towers, fortified by its surrounding walls. Next we went to Salamanca. This city was conquered by the Christians from the Moors in 1085. It reached world fame after the founding of the University in 1230 by Alfonso IX. It made Arabic philosophy accessible to the Western world. Throughout the Renaissance, it was the center of Spanish cultural life and Spanish theology. It was partially demolished by the French in 1811. it served as the capital for the insurgents during the Spanish Civil War (1936-1937).

We bought meat and cheese at a market and had a picnic on the grounds of the University, which has a richly adorned facade and contains precious manuscripts. Nearby was the most unique of the many splendid palaces, the Casa de las Conchas, named for the numerous scallop shells on its facade.

We were on our way to Portugal, crossing very mountainous country. I was reminded of Switzerland. All of the houses had tiny gardens in front, filled with flowers. Across the border lies Quarda, the highest town in Portugal, on the slopes of the Serra da Estrela. After passing through breathtaking landscape with deep valleys, we dropped down to a precious small hotel in Oliveira do Hospital, Portugal.

My room overlooked a church garden with olive trees and lupine. The dinner served at the hotel consisted of tasty potato soup and fish patties. I had the opportunity to practice my Portuguese, having lived in Brazil for two years. It came back very slowly, since many years had passed. The people I spoke with were most grateful for my trying to converse with them in their own language. As I struggled, we laughed boisterously at my mistakes.

We moved fast on these tours. The morning was to be spent visiting one of Portugal's oldest and most beautiful cities. Coimbra perches high above the Mondego river and its steep and tiered streets take you back to 1290 when its great university was founded. We walk through the open-air market with its colorful sights of fruit, vegetables, meats, live poultry, and crowds of people from the villages doing their shopping. I bought olives, tomatoes, and goat cheese for a picnic on a bus stop bench after walking through the park. One of our group got lost in the park. As soon as we found our lost friend, we dashed off again for Lisbon by way of Leiria, famous for its castle.

What a way to see everything, wandering all around Coimbra in the morning and arriving in Lisbon that same afternoon. After a gourmet dinner that evening of fish, chicken, and salad, we were treated to a show with fantastic music and dancing.

The next morning we never stopped. First we had a tour of the city of Lisbon, visiting the monument of Henry the Navigator who made this city the 15th Century mistress of the seas. He was the son of King John I of Portugal. The Iberian Peninsula, which is made up of Spain and Portugal, has the shape of a woman's head. She is facing west and her profile is the western coast of Portugal. At the tip of her chin, which is Cabo de São Vicente, we find Sagres. Henry founded a naval arsenal here and added an observatory and a school to study geography and navigation. One of his navigators rediscovered the Madeira Island and explored the west coast of Africa. Eventually, a slave trading post was established. His captains returned with slaves and gold. This caused the coast to become very popular. The abuses of the slave trade caused Henry to forbid the kidnapping of the negroes in 1455.

As we visited St. Jerome's Church, a funeral was going on. A coach museum was also on the agenda. Next, was a walk through the Alfama's tile decorated streets. This is a very old part of town. After a picnic, we went to Estoril and Cascais. We saw the mountains meet the ocean plus a castle in Sinta, as a bonus.

Leaving Lisbon we crossed the rolling plains of the Alentejo. This province in southeastern Portugal is drained by the River Guadiana. It is called "the Granary of Portugal." Here horses, cattle, hogs, grain, olives, and fruit thrive. After we passed through these plains with woodlands of cork and eucalyptus trees, we entered the blinding light of Andalusia, with its tidy white painted villages.

After a very long drive, we finally arrived in the splendid and colorful city of Seville. The next morning we had another bustling tour of a tobacco factory, the bullring, and the cathedral, which is the largest in Spain. We pushed on to the famous Giralda Tower with its intricate Moorish decoration, and to the 12th century Alcazar, which was once a Moorish Royal Palace.

A savory lunch of lamb chops, asparagus, and wine sent everyone off for a nap. When I awoke, I wandered out into the streets to find a church to photograph. The streets were empty. Not a soul was in sight. Evidently, they were having an extended siesta.

I found my church, and after taking several pictures, I ambled away. Suddenly, I heard someone behind me running very fast, with his shoes pounding on the sidewalk. It was a very handsome young Spaniard. He came right at me. I was stunned. He knocked me down and got my wallet with my money, my American Express Card, and my scuba diving card. I must have screamed, because instantly a crowd of people poured out of a nearby bar. They came to help and comfort me. They expressed shock and concern that a tourist had been treated this way. I had to go to the police station to report the incident. There, I met a Frenchman with a broken collar bone, who had been through the same experience. The American Express office cancelled my card and issued a new one immediately. They were very efficient. After I returned home, I was amazed when my cards were mailed to me from Spain. I treated myself to dinner at the hotel that night so I could watch the floor show.

We were on day eleven of seventeen. We had been at a rapid pace. Next was Morocco. Our coach followed the wide valley of the Guadalquivir River, passing through the famous sherry vineyards around Jerez. Then we went south, skirting the Costa de la Luz. Arriving in the busy port of Algeciras, we boarded the ferry, which took us across the Straits of Gibraltar to Ceuta. We didn't stop there. We headed for the enchanting city of Fez.

The following day was supposed to be leisurely while we investigate this ancient city of outstanding beauty, surrounded by many hills. There was no time for leisure. We wandered everywhere, including the Medina, an extremely old marketplace. There we watched the Berbers in flowing robes and their veiled women buy and sell their goods along the narrow pathways. I had the feeling I was in a strange other world, almost to the point of discomfort.

We loaded up again, the agenda being Meknes, Rabat, and Casablanca. The first stop was Meknes, the imperial city of Morocco, with its monumental gates, mosques, palaces, and huge protective walls. We went inside a mosque, after taking our shoes off.

We climbed back on the bus and headed for Rabat, the capital. We stayed one night there. Shortly after arriving, we drove to Casablanca on the Atlantic Ocean. Everyone was free to stroll wherever they wanted. Returning to Rabat, we were again free to wander through the wide boulevards, full of life.

Our next destination was Tangier, and then back to the Spanish mainland with a scenic drive along the Costa del Sol. We passed through Malaga and climbed up to Granada. Here there had been 800 years of Moorish reign, which finally ended the same year Columbus sailed for America. The city was immortalized by Washington Irving in his book *Tales of the Alhambra*. The Alhambra was built as a summer palace by the Moorish kings. Irving, a North American diplomat, historian, and traveler, actually lived for sometime in the Alhambra. It was here that he wrote his book, filled with color, atmosphere, firsthand impressions, humor and feeling, with a romantic outlook. We read of the legends and traditions which preserve today the charm and fascination of those years gone by. His book was published in 1832, and was immediately translated into many languages. Walking through the Alhambra was a magnificent experience.

The same afternoon we traveled northwards to the palm forests of Elche and on to Alicante. The next morning we flew to London and back to the United States. Our adventure had ended and it seemed like a fairy tale.

Russia—July 1987

The taxi couldn't find my house in Ahwatukee, but I finally made it to New York. Here I had to change terminals to catch the plane for London. After arriving, there was a three-hour wait for the Cosmos Tour Company to get organized and pulled together. Before I got off the plane, the person behind me dropped his heavy luggage on my shoulder. To this day, I shy away from the passengers taking their things out of the overhead bin.

On the way to London, the bus sideswiped a small car. There ensued a heated argument between the bus driver and the driver of the car. After arriving at the Hotel Royal Scott, we waited seven hours for a room to be available.

I intended to have only soup for dinner, but during the long wait, I got hungrier and hungrier. I ended up ordering pâté foie, lobster bisque, and lamb. It certainly wasn't gourmet. I took bread and the lamb for lunch the next day on the ferry from Dover to Ostend, Belgium.

The bus was leaving very early for Dover. It was cold and windy. When we left the hotel my ticket went blowing down the street before we boarded. I had to chase it.

We passed green rolling countryside with sheep. There were fields of hops and coal mines. Arriving in Dover, the harbor was beautiful with many ships and tons of traffic. The day was chilly with alternating sun and clouds. I ate the lamb sitting in the middle of the street on a turn-around object which held a large light post.

I met other tour passengers on the boat. We visited and fed the sea gulls. We were on the ferry four and a half hours.

We drove from Ostend to Ghent-Antwerp, arriving very late. Dinner was at the Belgium-Holland border. It was expensive. I paid nine dollars for a piece of ham, fish, and wine, There was quite a food layout which included mounds of raw hamburger. We arrived in Arnhem, Holland at one in the morning.

At 5:30 A.M. the bus rolled on toward Berlin. We passed forests and farms in the fog and rain. Lunch was on the East German border at Konigstotter. We had sandwiches made from the large assortment of meats and cheeses we had confiscated from the breakfast buffet.

There were three flags there: American, French, and English. Foreboding towers were occupied by guards with guns. The officials had grim, serious faces as they looked intently at our passport pictures and at the person holding the passport. They checked twice. It was still raining, and this added to the grimness of the uncomfortable situation. We were told that it was very difficult to leave East Germany. Only an urgent family matter would allow you to get permission to leave or crossover into the western sector of Berlin. As we entered Berlin, we underwent the same close scrutiny. Finally, we arrived at the hotel which was very nice. Our rooms overlooked a large gathering of protesting students called the Moon Group. We never found out what this demonstration was about.

We took off immediately for the city tour with our dark-haired female guide. We dashed along as she rattled off the points of interest with bits of historical events interjected. Finally, we stopped at the Berlin Wall. The wall is one hundred miles long and guarded by several thousand Grepos. There were paintings and signs on the wall. Some referred to people who had tried to get over, into Berlin, and had been shot and killed by the guards stationed in the surrounding towers. It was a very depressing sight, representing hopelessness and despair. Before the wall, two thousand a day came across to Berlin at Potsdamer Platz.

Our enthusiastic guide wanted us to know as much history as possible. It seems that Berlin was divided 800 years ago. It was just a coin trading town on the island in the River Spree. In 1307 no agreement could be reached among the factions. There was an increase in highwaymen, but in the 15th century, law was restored. In 1440 Berlin became an electoral residence for 500 years. From 1640-1688 there was a thirty year war. The population was diminished to 5000. Then there was a new boom of Heugonots in 1618-1648. These immigrants were French Protestants who fled to the Netherlands and Berlin in 1685. In 1707, Frederick III was King of Prussia. Under this king there was great development with great cultural and intellectual strides. Berlin was called the "Athens of the Spree." In 1870-1871, there was war with France. Otto Von Bismarck united Germany then with Kaiser Wilhelm, there was another great cultural growth. Berlin became a leading industrial city. In 1914-1918, World War I brought catastrophic events, with Wilhelm II fleeing to Holland.

In 1920, Berlin Law formed Berlin. There were eight cities, fifty-nine villages, and twenty-seven estates divided into twenty districts. Strikes, inflation, and unemployment brought Hitler in from 1933-1945. There were twelve years of terror called the "brown spook" which left rubble and fifty-six million dead.

At the time of my visit, there were two million in West Berlin and one million and two hundred thousand in East Berlin. There were twenty-two districts. The ones under the Soviets are called vodka, four under the British called whisky, two under the French called champagne, and the ones under American are called Coca-Cola. In the American sector there is a 2,400 foot waterfall Kreuzberg, the highest point in Berlin. Tiergarten Park with one million trees, is called the "green lung of Berlin." They say there are three trees for each dog.

There are many architectural points of interest such as the Kaiser Wilhelm Memorial Church and the Schonsberg Castle. The Reichstag Building, in Italian Renaissance, where the former houses of parliament were, was destroyed by arsonists in 1945. There is a Column of Victory two hundred and ten feet high with a Golden Victoria figure on top weighing 78,000 pounds. The Brandenburg Gate, the entrance to the city, was built in 1791.

There is a Memorial to Russian Soldiers which is guarded by two Russians at all times. The Airlift Memorial recalls the Russian Blockade of West Berlin, making it an island. Supplies were flown in dramatically. The Airlift was called Raisin Bombers, This occurred in 1948-1949. The Spandow Allied Prison had one prisoner, Rudolph Hess. He died while we were there, at the age of ninety-three.

The Germans make fun of the modern buildings. The Berliners call one "Compact," another "Hollow Tooth" and another "Lipstick." They have named one building "Jimmy Carter's Smile."

Our attractive German guide had several jokes she felt she must pass on to us. I think they were a standard part of her tour. Several examples were: Napoleon always wore a red shirt so men couldn't see the blood if he were shot. Now we know why Hitler always wore brown trousers. There are so many cars in West Berlin. Everyone in West Berlin has a car and everyone in East Berlin has a parking place.

Leaving Berlin and entering Poland, we underwent the same meticulous inspection at the border. They checked the passports numerous times, looking into our eyes. The baggage compartments were checked for items and persons. At the border I visited with a Polish man in French. We had lunch at Razpin.

My impression of Poland was an overwhelming old world feeling. There were crude rustic houses. It was very flat and agricultural with many crops, but there seemed to be no activity. No workers were seen. We stopped at Objazd, an industrial town.

General facts given by the bus guide were: men work until age 65 and women work until 55. They work two Saturdays a month. There are thirty--seven million in Poland. Before the war it was multinational, but now there are almost no minorities. It has 600 kilometers of sea coast. Twenty-two percent of the area is covered by forest where we find Polish bison, wild boars, deer, pheasants, geese, and ducks.

There are also many minerals such as coal, copper, zinc, lead, sulfur, and rock salt. The mines are 80% privately owned, 10% cooperatives and 10% collective. Big properties are divided with the largest being around thirty acres. The farmers supply the government with a certain percentage. They can sell the rest. The main crops are wheat, oats, barley, potatoes, sugar beets, and flax.

There is an extensive system of rivers: the River Elbe near Potsdam, West of Berlin; the River Spree in Berlin; the River Oder on the German Polish border.

Poland converted to Christianity in the 13th century. The Tartars and Mongols destroyed part of Poland in the 14th century war with the Teutonic Knights.

In January of 1945, Warsaw, Poland's capital since the 17th century, was a desert of ruin and rubble, a victim of systematic Nazi destruction. On the Warsaw tour, we saw the historic old quarters, the Palace of Culture and Sciences and the old town of Warsaw with walls on the River Vistula. We visited the old market place, Praga North. There was a priest who offered to die in the place of a man with a family. His picture was in the church. The man he saved was still alive at eighty. Parts of German war equipment were still embedded in the cathedral wall, as was a damaged cross.

The reconstructed plaza and market place had an elegant restaurant where we had lunch of mutton, potatoes, and carrots. They served an interesting salad. There was a whole boiled egg on lettuce, with peas, onions, tomato, and pimiento on top. Then there was a slice of ham over all of this garnished with parsley. Another was gelatin with diced chicken, peas, etc.

After lunch, I went shopping in a large department store for a comforter, but they would not take American Express or American money, so I went back to the hotel to exchange the money. I raised my skirt up at the desk to get at my money belt, but everyone was out to lunch. I gave up on my down comforter.

The group attended a Chopin recital in Schuster Castle on a magnificent piano. There was Chopin and champagne. This made up for the shopping disappointment. It was pouring down rain when we left the recital.

As we were getting ready to leave Poland for Russia, I met some Cubans in the lobby. I talked up a storm with them and yelled "Viva Cuba." They proudly gave me cards with pictures of Havana, Fidel Castro, and Che Guevarra.

We left early and had a breakfast picnic on the Polish-Russian border. My friend and I had a beer with the last of my Polish money. He hid his knife in the bag with my negligee.

On the way to the border, we passed small houses with charming little gardens in front, haystacks, and carts going to market. In Poland and Russia we were told not to drink the water. There were rest stops called "the bush-bush." That is where everyone took off for the bushes and trees for relief.

It took several hours to pass through the Polish officials and Russian officials. The Russians almost took the bus apart looking for stowaways and only the good Lord knows what else. They literally unscrewed many sections of the bus and then couldn't put it back together. The bus drivers were extremely irritated and almost came to blows.

One of the ladies on the tour tried to give a bar of soap as a present to a resident seen off in the bushes. The Russian was too afraid to come forward, so the woman left the soap on a large rock for her to retrieve.

We finally crossed into Russia at Brest, a frontier town, to the boisterous music of the Volga Boatman. It used to be a fortress near the Sostand Forest.

Russia was the biggest continent in the world, two continents separated by the Ural Mountains. It had eleven zones. Syvodnick is where they work a whole day extra for no money. The money goes for bettering the country. The civil war took the country back to the 1890's. In 1929 the five year plan started against starvation. There was a boom in construction with the pick and shovel workers. In 1932 the first trucks were produced. In 1939 they put the first man into space. In World War II, fifty million people were killed.

Byelorussia (White Russia) has many lakes. Ten million people live here. Flax and potatoes are the primary crops. The name "white" came from the linen clothes and the fair-haired light skinned people living on the land. The Slavic tribes united. Byelorussia was occupied by German tribes. In 1919 Polish troops advanced and occupied this area. They retreated to Minsk and Byelorussia ceded to the Poles but was reunited in 1929. The Nazis destroyed 209 of the 270 cities. After the war, there was complete reconstruction.

Minsk is capital of six regions. There are many trees in this area. A soup is made from the sap of the Birch tree. In all of the wooded areas, there are oryx and bison. Only the Russian Czar could hunt here. The last oryx was killed in 1919. Five were brought from Germany, and now there are 150 oryx, many deer, beavers, badgers, reindeer, and storks—black storks. The storks used to be white and very friendly toward people. Then a woman took a black frying pan and started to strike a stork. The legend is the bird turned black immediately and went into the forest. Now they are all black.

There are many swamps (polesia). Thirty percent of all Byelorussia is marsh and swamps cover sixty percent. They tried to dry them up, using a strong wind and today twenty percent is made up of swamps with twelve percent heavy peat. In the drained areas are collective farms. Potatoes are the main crop. There are over five hundred recipes. One is a mixture of grated raw potato, onion, salt, pepper, and soda dropped on hot greased pans and served with sour cream. This mixture is also baked. In white Russia, there are women living who are over one hundred years old.

Our first day in Minsk, we had a city tour. Our hotel, the Planet, was enormous, sitting on a hill overlooking the city and a large monument that was called the Union of Socialists Republic Victory 1944--1945. Of the two hundred eighty million people in all of Russia, only nineteen million are communists.

What I remember about the hotel is that the shower curtains were too short and the water got all over the floor. The bath towels were extremely small. The maid raved about my peasant skirt and silver Concho belt. We hugged each other and I learned to say "thank you"—"spicebo." The hotel was huge and very quiet and dark. Breakfast consisted of hardboiled eggs in a large bowl.

My impressions of the city were that it was large and modern in some aspects, but crude in others. No one was in the streets.

The monument across from the hotel was a large obelisk with a gold star and fern on top. There was a black statue of a woman with trumpets in her hand. We were taken to another statue with fountains, honoring the poet Cupala. The statues of two huge women were in the fountains casting wreaths into the water. According to folklore, in June, on the shortest night, the man goes to the forest to find flowers of the fern. This guarantees his happiness. The women go to find the fern alone and make two wreaths. They float them in the water. If the wreaths meet, there will be marriage and happiness, If one wreath sinks, they try again the next year.

We visited another victory monument in the city. It was another obelisk with a star at the top. There was a perpetual flame and many guards in front. A uniformed youth guard changes every twenty minutes. We watched the change.

Leaving Minsk in the afternoon, we saw the same forests and rolling farms. There were patches of wild heather along the side of the road. It was raining. We passed through Borisoc on the bank of the Berezina River. During the retreat of Napoleon in 1812, this city was destroyed. Again it was demolished by the Nazis. We saw the mounted Nazi tank that was the first to enter. The whole situation was gloomy. There was lots of traffic making it impossible to pass. The only pleasant part was the music from *Dr. Zhivago* the bus driver was playing.

We arrived at the 1100 year old city of Smolensk on the Dnieper River. It is a beautiful town situated on hills, with many lovely churches. It is called "the Gateway to Moscow." In 1596 there was a Medieval wall six and one-half kilometers long and twelve meters high. Three horses could ride abreast on top of this wall.

Our guide explained that church and state are separate and each person could follow the religion of his choice. The exact number of believers was unknown, but an estimate was ten to fifteen percent. There were forty-two religious organizations and sixteen functioning monasteries. In 1918, all church property of the Russian Orthodox and others were confiscated.

In the morning, we had a city tour. The Cathedral of Assumption was started in 1677 and finished in 1740. During the Napoleon invasion, there was no damage to the walls of the Cathedrals, but the Nazis left it standing with no roof nor windows. We attended a service. There were very few people. Mostly women dressed in drab dark clothing were standing about, as is the custom. The priests, with black beards and long robes, conducted the service while standing behind a wall, On the collection plate there were many American dollars.

It had rained all night, but I had a lovely room by myself with open windows. From a window I could see the wind blowing the fir trees. There was even hail. The next morning was very cold with wind and rain. It did not seem like August. Drab little old ladies were sweeping around the hotel with brooms made of twigs and brush. They were not at all pleased when I tried to photograph the scene.

Our guides never stopped talking for long. They briefed us on as much of the history of Russia as they could. This was a running monologue as we traveled along. It was fragmented, so I have tried to add some details to clarify the notes I took on the bus.

Russian history is like a long arduous tug-of-war between eastern (Asian) and western (European) forces. Since ancient times, through brutal and bloody combat, one group and then the other gained control.

Some important dates may help us to orient ourselves. In 800 A.D. the first Russian state was established in Kiev. In 988 A.D., Valdimir I converted Russia to Christianity, but in 1237-1240 A.D. the Mongols conquered Russia. The Mongols were Asiatic people from Mongolia and Manchuria. Their traits were slanted eyes, high cheek bones and yellow pigmentation. They were predominantly pastoral people, and generally Llamist Buddhists. The Mongolian hordes who conquered Russia penetrated as far as Hungary, Germany, and Turkey. They came to be known as Tartars. They destroyed one town after another, including Kiev in 1240. During the Mongol period, which ended in the 1400's, Russia was cut off from the Renaissance spirit occurring in Western Europe.

During the 1300's, Prince Yuri of Moscow married the sister of the Golden Horde's Khan (ruler). One Russian prince became Ivan I in 1330. He was allowed to collect taxes and became a great landowner. Moscow became the spiritual center of Russia. It also became stronger and richer, but the Golden Horde became weaker. In 1380, the Grand Prince Dimitri defeated the Mongol force, but in 1382 the Mongols re-captured Moscow.

In the region of the Ukraine, the Germanic tribes—called the Goths—conquered the area about 200 A.D. where they ruled until 370 A.D. These were the Visigoths or Western Goths. The pressure of the invasion by the Huns threw the Goths into confusion. These warlike, nomadic, pastoral people from Asia undertook military campaigns, living off the countries they ravaged. Military superiority was due to their small rapid horses on which they appeared to be glued. Attila was their greatest king, and their empire broke up after he died in 453 A.D. The Avars, related to the Huns, ruled in the mid 500's. In the mid 600's the Khazars of Asia won the southern Volga and the northern Caucasus regions, and became Jews.

In the 800's, Slavic groups came in and established towns in what is now known as European Russia. No one knows where the Slavs came from.

The earliest Russian history was the Primary Chronicle. It dealt with the 800's and was written in Kiev around 1111 A.D. It claims that quarreling Slavic groups in Novgorod asked a Viking tribe to rule and bring order. The Vikings were called Varangian Russes. It is believed that this is where Russia got its name. Related Varangian families headed by Rurik arrived in 862, when they settled in Novgorod. The area was known as "Land of the Rua." It is concluded that the first Russian state was established in Kiev during the 800's.

Kiev lay on the main route, connecting the Baltic Sea to the Black Sea and the Byzantine Empire. About 988 the Grand Prince Valdimir I became a Christian, as has been mentioned earlier. He was baptized in Constantinople (Istanbul). The Russians were pagans, worshipping idols representing the forces of nature. Valdimir made Christianity the state religion and became a saint in the Russian Orthodox Church.

There were numerous destructive civil wars in Novgorod and other towns. Kievan Russia fell to the Mongolian hordes during the 1200's.

I have investigated a few of the most outstanding ruler's of Russia, famous and infamous, which I believe deserve to be mentioned.

Ivan III, The Great, (1440-1505) opened the way for a unified Russia. He freed Russia in 1480 from the 240 years rule by the Tartars. He extended his rule over adjoining territories and the great trading town of Novgorod was added. He strengthened his rule over the church and the nobles, revising Russian law code. He was known for his prudence and wisdom. He married Sophia, the niece of the last Byzantine emperor.

Ivan IV, The Terrible, (1530-1584) ruled fifty-one years as Czar of Russia. He was the first to be called czar. He was brutal, extremely suspicious, and thought to be insane by many. He formed a special police force. There was a reign of terror with the arrest and murder of hundreds of aristocrats. He burned many towns and villages and killed church leaders who opposed him. He was crafty and cruel. In a fit of rage, he struck and killed his own son. He was married seven times. When he wished to dispose of a wife, he forced her to become a nun.

Ironically, he ranks next to Peter the Great, as the most outstanding czar. He crossed the Ural Mountains and conquered western Siberia and then took over the region along the Volga River. He made Moscow the capital, and reduced the nobles, ministers, merchants, and farmers to servants of the czar. He and later czars passed laws that held the peasants to the land as serfs, while serfdom was disappearing in western Europe. He published a new law code and introduced new administrative systems called Oprichina. This made everything subject to the czar alone. He did, however, invite experts from other countries to improve Russian craftsmanship and military techniques. He also began diplomatic relations and trade with the western powers.

Ivan's son, Theodore I, was mentally incompetent and a weak czar. His wife's brother Boris Godunov, became the ruler. Theodore died in 1598.

Russia was torn by civil war and invasion. There was political confusion until 1613, when Michael Romanov became czar. This started the Romanov line of czars who ruled for three hundred years, until the Revolution of 1917. Romanov was the name adopted in the 16th century by a family of great nobles that traced its origin to the 14th century. Ivan IV, took, as his first wife, Anastasia Romanov. Alexis, the son and direct successor of Michael, ruled from 1645 until 1676. Then Feodor III, son of Alexis, was czar until 1682. Although he was an invalid, Feodor III tried to carry out reforms. Other children fathered by Alexis and his first wife were Sophia and the semi-imbecile, Ivan. Peter I was the youngest child of Alexis by his second wife.

Peter I or Peter the Great, as he is better known (1682-1725), was a man of astounding energy and vision. He was relentless and many times ruthless in his determination to expand and modernize Russia. He rightly deserved to be called "The Great," this depending on one's definition of "great." He has gone down in history to be greatly remembered for his radical ambitions and the lengths to which he went to realize them.

Peter and Ivan V, his feeble minded half brother, were co-czars as children. Ivan's sisters Sophia, ruled as regent until 1689. When Ivan died in 1696, Peter came into full power and became czar, at which time, it was reported that Sophia was plotting his death. Peter overthrew the regent with the help of his supporters.

There had been bloody disorder between the two factions, one supporting Ivan and the other supporting ten year old Peter. During this time, one of Peter's chief supporters was cut into pieces while clutching the child's sleeve. This is thought to have caused permanent psychological damage, causing Peter to suffer convulsive fits.

Peter spent most of his childhood in virtual exile with friends from the rough social element. His talent for leadership became apparent from the start when he organized military games.

As czar, he had a great interest in building a navy and modernizing the army. He made close contact with western Europe and continued his shipbuilding experiments. He realized that Russia needed better maritime outlets, so he expanded Russia's territory to the Baltic Sea, controlled by Sweden. His ambition was to also go to the Black Sea, controlled by Turkey.

He set off on a tour of western Europe, traveling incognito much of the time. He studied European industrial techniques, even working as a carpenter in the shipyards of Holland. Then he was called back to Russia by a military revolt instigated by Sophia. He took drastic and sadistic vengeance on his opponents. He started a reform program by personally cutting off the beards of many nobles. The beards were social symbols of medieval Russia.

Eventually, he began the northern war against Sweden (1700-1721) which controlled the Baltic Sea. His hope was to control the Black Sea, then under Turkey. He retained most of his numerous ambitious conquests, however he lost most of the territory he had fought for in Turkey.

Other changes which Peter I brought about were: he moved the capital from Moscow to St. Petersburg; introduced taxation; unified the currency; freed women from their servile status; ordered the building of stone houses; and established fire departments to stop the extensive disastrous fires in the wooden cities.

The list of his endeavors is never-ending. He abolished the Byzantine court ritual introduced by Sophia, the second wife of Ivan III and niece of the last Byzantine emperor. He simplified the alphabet, reformed the calendar, encouraged the rise of private industry and expansion of trade, and built the first modern hospital and medical schools in Russia. He wanted Russians to wear European type clothing instead of the Russian garments.

He completely reorganized religion and government drastically, however he did nothing to restrict serfdom which became even more entrenched. He tried to enforce all of his reforms with severity, but he was unable to do away with the corruption nor was he able to force the Western ways on the peasants. His reforms met widespread opposition.

The conservatives within the clergy, accused him of being the Antichrist. His own son, Alexis, part of the opposition, was tried for treason and died in 1718 from being tortured.

He proclaimed himself "Emperor of all Russia" in 1721. In 1722, he banished imperial succession by primogeniture, instead, leaving the choice of the successor up to the sovereign. Catherine I, a Livonian peasant girl whom Peter had made his mistress and then later his wife, succeeded him.

His reign revolutionized Russia. Before he came into power, Russia was—compared to Europe—a remote Asiatic country. After his death, it was one of the major European powers.

His personal traits ranged from bestial cruelty and vice to a strong devotion to duty. He was of enormous stature and had the strength of Hercules, being able to drink himself into a stupor and indulge in various vices, while still able to rise up at a moment's notice to withstand great physical exertion and privation, which was what he expected from his subjects. Unfortunately, not many had his stamina, and thousands died unnecessarily on his projects, including the building of St. Petersburg.

He was driven by an obsession to improve the welfare of the state and to enforce reforms as soon as possible, even by ruthless means. He believed that for the Russian people to accomplish anything, they had to be prodded. The paradox is that the man who introduced the western ways into Russia with such passion, was himself regarded by his contemporaries in western Europe as the incarnate of Russian barbarism. Peter eventually died of his excesses in 1725.

The tour arrived in Moscow for Saturday and Sunday sightseeing. The enormous Ukraine Hotel was where we lodged.

First, there was a city tour of Red Square and St. Basil's Cathedral. Basil was a beggar, and it was believed that beggars were closer to the church, so he was buried in the church which bore his name. This is an architectural marvel, with eight onion domes. We saw Lenin's tomb with the never-ending line which forms everyday. These are people who want to look at Lenin's face. He has been preserved in a very special way.

There was the Bolshoi Theatre and the Moscow State University located very high on Sparrow Hill, overlooking the Moscow River. The University dates from 1775, the oldest of fifty-five in the country. It is built on seven hills and the wind was extremely gusty. We saw eight to ten wedding parties coming to take pictures for good luck.

Across the river, looking towards the Kremlin, we saw numerous churches. This created an unusual skyline from left to right: a tall bell tower, the Church of Peter The Great, the Church of the Archangel Michael and the Cathedral of Annunciation. We passed by Luzhniki Park, Europe's biggest sports complex.

Finally, on the Kremlin tour, we walked around the grounds, the bell tower and other monuments to Ivan The Great. We saw the Queen of the Belle and the King of Cannons monuments.

The Kremlin Palace joins a church on one side and on the other side is the Parliament. Kremlin means fortress or citadel and dates from the late 14th century. The guides took us to the Assumption of Mary Church which was filled with icons. In the same area was the Czar's Bell with a big chunk missing out of it, and an extremely ornate cannon.

We entered the Metro. It was immaculate and artistically decorated. We examined the five stations or levels. Each one was decorated differently. There were elaborate works of marble, mosaics, stained glass, and carvings. The many kinds of marble held golden flowers. The last level was modern, filled with red marble from the Ural Mountains. There were numerous bright white oval pictures on the coiling, many depicting airspace.

Sunday we had a church service in the hotel room. It was touching. Then off we went to the Exhibition of Economic Achievement. This is a large park with seventy pavilions showing the achievements of the USSR after the Revolution. The Cosmos Pavilion, or Space Pavilion, contained full-scale models of Sputniks.

In the Exhibition we found one pavilion filled with the crafts of children. There was magnificent handwork in leather, pottery, and metal.

On the grounds were ornate fountains decorated with gold and silver, and beautiful buildings with richly carved facades. An enormous space monument soared into the sky with a rocket on top.

In the Lenin Museum, we saw a film on Lenin, who still has many worshippers. His statues and pictures were everywhere, even though he has been dead since 1924. On display was the clothing of his wife and the coat he was wearing when he was shot. There were red and white x's where the bullets went through. He survived this experience.

Later, I wandered through the streets and found a bookstore where I browsed and bought three beautiful books.

We were not able to get into the Circus that evening, but went to a folklore and modern dance performance, which was excellent.

We left Moscow and again had to drive to another hotel for breakfast because it was so early on a Monday morning. It was raining. As we traveled, we passed many villages, large lakes, and very unique houses with small colorful gardens in front of the house and windows. They resembled gingerbread houses. We passed the Volga River and went through the charming town of Kalin where Tschaikowsky had lived and composed much of his music.

Novgorod was our next stop. Situated on the River Volkhov, it is one of Russia's oldest towns. It is mentioned for the first time in the Primary Chronicle, written around 1111 A.D. In the 9th century, it was a principality and in the 12th century, a united medieval. In the 13th century, Russia suffered devastations, but Novgorod did not. Ivan III annexed it to Russia. In 1611-1617, there was intervention by Sweden. It was captured by the Nazis in 1941. Twenty-nine mosques were destroyed. Two hundred thousand people lived there at the time of our visit. It is a chemical and electronic center now. It has medieval architecture. We visited the 18th century Kremlin and the Sophia Cathedral with its many icons. There were many Romanesque churches built from the 12th through the 16th centuries. St. Paraskeva and St Phillip are still functioning. Aspen shingles were used, which look like silver in the sun.

On the city tour we saw the frescoes of St. Sofia, the Last Supper icons and the Festival Bell. The story goes that Ivan The Terrible was on his horse crossing a bridge. The bell rang so loudly that his horse roared up and he almost fell into the river. He ordered the ears to be cut off of the boy who rang the bell, as well as the ears of the bell itself. This story may be true as the top was cut off of the bell.

They used to stand on the bridge over the river and judge the guilty. They threw the suspected criminal into the river and if he sank, they said: "The river accepted him, so we are right." If he swam to shore, they said: "The river won't have him, we are still right."

I made a few general observations in this town. The houses were decorative with colorful gardens. The women were all poorly dressed wearing bandanas on their heads, while they walked their cows, goats, and sheep by the side of the road.

One morning at breakfast, I put a boiled egg into each pocket of my white skirt. The one in my right pocket broke, making a terrible mess. I continued my walk with bright yellow yolk all over my right side. In the street, I met a little boy with his dog. I took his picture and asked him for his address so I could send a picture to him. One of those drab women quickly passed near to him, speaking lowly. He ran away.

On our way to Leningrad, we passed through a pastoral countryside with herds of cattle. There were sleek black cattle lying scattered throughout the fields.

We entered Leningrad, founded in 1703, and finished in 1712. It was built on the Neva River, on one hundred and one islands twenty-five miles from the ocean, by Peter the Great. Neva is the Swedish word for mud. It was constructed on stilts or piles. There are thirty-five gracefully arched bridges spanning more than two hundred miles of waterway within the city. Twenty thousand workmen were conscripted to build it. Many died on the job. Peter made Petrograd (Leningrad) the capital, which Moscow had a hard time accepting. It is a smaller city than Moscow and more European, having much more culture than Moscow. It is more of a museum than a metropolis. The Cathedral, also built by Peter, is the highest in the world.

The points of interest on the city tour were the Winter Palace behind the Column of Alexander, the Fortress of Peter and Paul and the St. Isaac Cathedral. In addition were the two Arches of Triumph and the Academy of Fine Arts. The Hermitage Palace is filled with many sculptures and other treasures imported by Catherine II. Nevski Prospekt is the most elegant avenue in Leningrad.

In 1617, Sweden came in and occupied this area. In 1700, Peter I (The Great) launched his twenty-one year war. In 1703, the land went back to St. Petersburg, then called Petrograd. Then, in World War II, Leningrad was besieged for 900 days and destroyed. This included the Hermitage Palace.

Catherine II, The Great, was the czarina from 1762-1796. She appeared from virtual obscurity from Anhalt-Zerbst, a former state in central Germany. Her name was Sophie, but was changed to Catherine, when an arrangement was made for her to become the wife of Peter III. He was the son of Anna Petrovna, daughter of Peter The Great. She was extremely powerful, creating a strong bureaucracy and an imperialistic foreign policy. Her reign began in 1762, only after a conspiracy led by Grigori Orlov, one of her numerous lovers. Catherine, dressed in a guard's uniform, participated in the forcing of

Peter to sign his abdication. A few days later he died, believed to have been assassinated.

She read widely, having an intimate relationship with Voltaire. She, herself wrote extensively, stories and comedies in French and Russian. She was behind much warfare and annexation, such as in Crimea and the partition of Poland. The colonization of Alaska happened during her reign Despite her enlightenment, the serfs were left in worse condition than before.

Catherine's son Paul, reigned five years and then was assassinated in 1801. Alexander I, Paul's son and a handsome czar, was throned and defeated Napoleon in 1812.

The Hermitage was reconstructed as a museum in Neo-Greek style in the 19th century from the original pavilion palace erected by Catherine II. It is filled with treasures she imported, such as the rarest of Greek jewelry from the Crimea. It is rich in French and Spanish paintings, including a number of Rembrandts. We spent several hours wandering through this fantastic collection.

Next, was St. Isaac's Cathedral, famous for its stained glass, wood carvings, gilt, and icons. In the Palace Square, stands the largest obelisk in the world. It is all in one piece of granite, held in place by its own weight. In Smolny Square, we see a large red building built for Catherine's son, Paul. When Paul was assassinated, it was turned over to a writing school, which Dostoevsky attended.

On our last day in Leningrad, I went shopping with another lady from the tour. We met at the Europe Hotel, which had at one time been elegant with marble. Now it was dirty and run-down with no toilet paper in the "johns." It was a cold, windy day, even in the middle of August. We took a long walk, looking into drugstores and a butcher shop where a stack of chickens were lying on a block. The customers had to go there, pick out a chicken, and put it in their own plastic bag. There were only three kinds of lunch meat. All of the stores were dismal and long lines formed at each one. There was no selection and all were antiquated.

We stayed in a fairly new hotel on the outskirts of town, but it was poorly constructed and not kept up. There was no hot water. The dining room was bright and had colorful objects hanging about, and there was a band. I danced with an attractive young man from Finland and with a friend from our tour group.

The next morning, we climbed on our bus, which had been nicknamed "Cucumber Express"' or the "Bush-Bush Bus." We said goodbye to Tanya, our guide, and prepared to leave Russia. Tears came to my eyes.

The hotel had prepared our lunches, wrapped in brown paper. There was a big piece of beef, lunch meat, two big pieces of cheese, four pickles, and boiled eggs. I saved mine until we got to Finland. There I sat at an outside table at a beautiful cafe with a bottle of wine and my brown paper Russian lunch.

At the border, before leaving Russia, we were delayed for over two hours. Again, the Russians meticulously examined the bus, removing panels and unscrewing many things, which they really screwed up because they couldn't get it all put back together again. Martin, the driver, was furious and finally grabbed one Russian by the arm, expressing his anger.

One of our passengers, the lady with the soap, would not give up. She went off into the woods on the other side of the street, trying again to carry some perfumed soap to a peasant woman. She was led back by an angry Russian soldier. It was hilarious to see her coming out of the "Bush-Bush" with the soldier.

Finland was a complete change. It was so clean. We saw the same forests and purple flowers, but there was more relief with large boulders along the edge of the forest. There were many more pine trees and less birch. Everything was well kept.

As a point of interest, provided by the guide, Finland was the only country that paid its debts to the United States from World War I. The country is Roman Catholic. It shares a border of thirteen thousand kilometers with Russia. The national industries, mostly exported, are fishing and ship building. It has two languages. Finnish is an Indo-Hungarian dialect. All of the signs are in Swedish and Finnish. An example is Helsinki, which is Finnish, and Aelsinfors, which is Swedish, for the same town. It is a Republic, and there are twelve political parties with elections every three years. It was occupied by Sweden in the 7th century. There is a communist party.

We stayed in the Hotel Espoo. It was beautiful, there were brightly colored chiffon drapes across the ceilings in the bar and dining room. In complete contrast to Russia, it was such a cheerful setting. The food was excellent. I hiked over to a cliff near the hotel, and looked at the rocks. I collected several granite specimens. There was wild heather here also.

We had our usual city tour. The guide always provided bits and pieces of unrelated information which resembled a sort of mosaic. Finland must be grateful to the German born architect, Carl Ludwig Engel and his partner, Ehrenstrom, for rebuilding the city after the great fire of 1808. The South Harbor and the cathedral, dominating Senate Square in the neoclassical style, were on the agenda. After passing the monument to composer Jan Sibelius and the Rock Church, we shopped in the colorful market square.

Helsinki is a large ship-building center. Many ships have been built here for Norway and the United States. We passed the flea market and the opera house. The film "Gorki Park" was made here. In 1710 there was a plague and twenty-one hundred people died. We saw the park where they were buried in mass, as were those who died in their civil war.

The average salary is two thousand dollars a month, with some making only thirteen hundred. However, taxation is 30%-80%. The universities are free of charge, as are the schools, including pencils and books.

We ate lunch in the train station on a bench with two blacks. They were going to school in Russia, and were completely disenchanted. It was cold and rainy—not pleasant. We walked around a market and climbed steep stairs to a large church.

That evening we sailed on the *Silvia Regina* ferry, a beautiful Swedish ship. Before dinner, a friend and I went up on the deck and watched the ship pull out. The harbor was sparkling with many colored lights. Later, there was a fantastic smörgâsbord set up. I have never seen so much food. There were large stacks of every kind of fish, caviar in huge bowls, a platter heaped with Lox salmon, rare roast beef, chicken, turkey, meatballs, and every kind of vegetable and salad. Then came the colossal desserts.

We were on the boat all night without sleeping accommodations. I slept about two hours on a couch with two Italians, Carlos and Mario, on other couches nearby. We visited and laughed at the young people who passed by all night long, getting louder and more drunk. It was pathetic. I went to the "john" at four A.M., came back, and someone was asleep on my couch. I wandered upstairs and visited with a Finnish boy who spoke perfect English. We watched an older couple sleeping on the floor, making out, He kept putting his hands in her slacks which crept down so low you could see her rear end. The Finn bought beers from the man when he woke up and I had a beer with the Finn at five in the morning. I needed one to shake off the experiences of the night.

The drunk was so hilarious. He said he was a navy man and his ship had sunk. The young Finn said that he was a typical Finnish sailor. The sailor said that where the ship sank was only a meter deep. Then he changed it to four meters. We died laughing. I remarked that things were getting worse.

We landed in Stockholm, but I was so tired I could hardly move. I had paid for two tours, so I gritted my teeth and proceeded. After a drive to the Katharina-Berget view of the city, we-strolled through the cobbled streets of the old city. We visited the main cathedral and the crystal fountain.

Next, we had an extensive tour of the town hall in which there is one famous room with mosaics containing eighteen million pieces of twenty-four karat gold. This is where the annual dinner for the Nobel Peace Prize winners takes place.

We trudged over to Skansen Park and the *Wasa* ship, which had been the pride of the Swedish fleet. On August 10, 1628, the *Wasa* sank in the harbor of Stockholm. Rediscovered in 1956, the world's oldest identified ship was finally raised in 1961. We climbed all around in it. There were extravagant wood carvings all over. It is made of oak wood. The *Wasa* ship was on the bottom of the sea for three hundred and thirty-three years before it was raised.

On our way back, we passed in the street an open manhole with the cover being held up by a statue. There was no explanation.

We were still having rain. A couple asked a young boy: "Does it always rain here?" He answered: "I don't know. I'm only eight years old."

We watched the changing of the guard at the palace. This very old city is built on fifteen islands.

Sweden has ninety-six thousand lakes, and is 90% forests and 9% lakes. It has a population of over eight million. It is at about the same latitude as Greenland, and there are traces of the last ice age. Eight to twelve thousand years ago the last glacier melted. Pre-Cambrian granites are the bedrocks. Mountain ranges to the northwest are of the Tertiary Period, Mountains were formed, and glaciers deposited boulders and dug holes. Six thousand feet is the highest elevation in Sweden. The rivers are used for transport. There are twenty-five provinces.

On our way to Denmark, we passed many green forests, red and white American-looking farm buildings, many lakes, and white churches. We saw other little houses with grass on the roof for insulation. We were told that if the grass needed to be cut a goat was put up on the roof.

If you sell a farm in this place, trees are put up as an indication. For a year, the person can buy back the farm. They plant one tree out alone and each day give it a beer to keep the previous owner away.

We had lunch on a lake, basking in warm sunshine by a pool. Then there was a twenty minute ferry ride over to Denmark. The harbor was picturesque.

Our guides persisted in telling jokes. Some went a little over my head, but I can't resist including them in the hope that someone might get it. Two gentlemen were in a bar one a Swede and the other Norwegian. Someone asked: Is that the moon or the sun?" The Norwegian said: "It is the sun." The Dane appeared and he was asked the same question. He said: "I don't know, I'm not from here."

Denmark is the smallest country between the Baltic and the North Seas. It includes the Faroe Islands. It is windy and very cold during the winters. There has always been a monarchy, and there is a shortage of natural resources. Nineteen percent of the land is agricultural. It is the second largest producer of beer and supplies many dairy products. Copenhagen dates from 1145. Many buildings are of the Dutch Renaissance. Its name translates as "harbor of merchants."

A story is told about the author Hans Christian Anderson. Whenever he went to bed, he left a note saying: "I'm not dead yet." He carried a rope everywhere he went in case there was a fire.

A friend and I wandered through Tivoli Gardens with its exquisite display of flowers. All through the park there were various stages set up, each one with a different show. My most poignant memory is of the delicate sculpture of the Little Mermaid by Edward Ericson. It was near the water's edge. I believe it is the most filmed object in Copenhagen. I had just run out of film, but I asked a friend to take a picture for me.

On our way home, we left Denmark in a pouring rain, passing through dark wet forests with little houses peeking out of the trees. My thoughts lingered on Copenhagen. I found it British in appearance. There was a drabness about it. The center of town was interesting and the Tivoli Gardens beautiful, but I felt a gloom settle over me as we drove on, in the fog. Bright yellow farmhouses were intersected by rows of trees. Other low, drab houses hugged the ground. A little white house appeared with trim that looked like a red vest. The rolling countryside continued, looking much like California. Small lakes and patches of yellow flowers cheered me for a moment. Then Dutch-like houses, with dark panels, built close to the ground emerged. Moss was growing on the roofs. Sheep and horses flourished. We drove into deep forests. Suddenly, a small pink church, trimmed in white with abundant gardens materialized. These were the surprises that counteracted the dismal.

One hour on a ferry and we were on the largest island of West Germany. We saw flat farm country with rows of trees marching across the background. We were following a hay truck. The hay flew into us. It was a fierce hay storm.

We arrived in Lubeck, Germany, a busy port and industrial town. We proceeded on to London to catch our flights home. We drove six thousand two hundred and six kilometers.

Spring Break—1988

I headed for Puerto Vallarta, Mexico in April. There was the usual inexpensive hotel and the daily visits to the beach. I ambled all over the city and rode city buses looking for biology posters in Spanish for my classes. Many of my students were from Mexico. I searched the restaurants hoping to find Cabrito, the baby goat. I had some success in both endeavors.

The evenings were spent sitting on the outdoor patio, listening to the Mexican band. I got to know three young teenage boys who worked keeping up the pool. They joined me at my table and we became good friends.

I signed up for a tour. The night before the tour, I was visiting with the boys I had met. I had my wallet on the table. A security guard from the hotel approached us. I thought he knew the boys. I turned my head for a few minutes, talking to my friends, and when I got to my room I discovered my wallet had been stolen with $135.00 cash in it. It could only have been the security guard, but the hotel could not help me. No tour!! I had to spend my time in an American Express office. This was not a happy ending.

Los Cabos—July 1988

 Well, I didn't give up. There I was, at the Hotel Palmilla in Los Cabos, Mexico. This was a beautiful hotel, right on the beach with the waves crashing in around tremendous boulders. It was a wonderful experience. There was a picturesque outdoor eating area with excellent food. I met many nice people with whom I visited.

 One day, I walked a good mile to the nearby bay to snorkel, only to discover that my new mask was not functioning. Still, this was a relaxing vacation compared to Puerto Vallarta, where I was robbed.

 I had one evening of excitement when a beautiful little bird flew into my room. He entered through the open doors of the verandah. I gently chased him all over the bathroom, hoping to steer him toward the opening. He finally escaped after I had taken several photos of him.

Honduras—December 1988

At last I was going to Tegucigalpa, Honduras, and Costa Rica. I had been fascinated, completely captivated by the name Tegucigalpa ever since the Alaskan cruise with my mother in 1983. That's a long time to dream about a place. The plane came in between high mountains, one of which had a huge Coca-Cola sign in neon lights on its flank.

At the high school where I was teaching, one of my students was a young girl from Tegucigalpa. She asked me to take some clothes down to her family. I bought an expandable suitcase and went by her apartment. We loaded the suitcase with clothes until we could barely zip it up. I checked this suitcase through with my luggage.

The first thing I did upon landing was to try and find a taxi driver to help me locate the family of my student so I could deliver the clothes. All of the taxis were gathered around on the incline leading out of the airport. We had the typical wrangling over the price. I was too tired to argue. I chose Carlos with his little beige Toyota and paid him six dollars. We had a very difficult time, but found the poor barrio where the family lived. There were no paved streets, only rain-gutted dirt roads. It was an emotional encounter. They were elated upon receiving word from their daughter and thrilled with the clothes. We unpacked the suitcase and I carried it to my hotel.

That evening, I went down to the bar to listen to the music. They served delicious little sandwiches of ham and cream cheese. The men in the bar were overly boisterous. I escaped to the restaurant to have a huge bowl of black bean soup, then I retired, but could not sleep. The traffic went on all night with horns blasting. People moved about in the street And music throbbed from the bars. I watched numerous drunken fights in the doorways below, visible from my window.

The next morning, I investigated many streets on foot. What a picturesque city it was! At last I found a travel agency. I wandered in and told a young lady, Luz, that I wanted to see everything I could for the least amount of money. She prepared an agenda which included Copán with its famous Mayan ruins, San Pedro Sula, La Ceiba, and Costa Rica.

She had me taking public buses all ever Honduras. I made my way to the Hedman bus station, only to find there were no buses leaving until 3:00 P.M. I waited from 11:30 till 3:00. It was Christmas-time and all the buses were jammed. When each bus arrived there was a terrible jostle getting on. I watched one after another fill up and drive away, At last, with the help of a young girl, I got on.

Luz had told me to get off at Chamelecón, merely a wide spot in the road. Here I had to take another bus to the entrance of the Copán Ruins. We had left Tegucigalpa so late, because of the Christmas crowds. By the time I arrived at this place to leave my bus, it was dark. I walked across the road in front of the bus, carrying my luggage, with great difficulty. As I watched my bus pull away, I learned that the last bus had left for the Copán Entrada. The hotel did not exist. I was desperate. I stuck out my thumb and hitchhiked. Two strangers in a van offered to take me on the two hour ride to a very small town that night where there was a hotel, of sorts. I would have to take another bus the next morning at 4:00 A.M. to arrive at the ruins.

These men were gentlemen. They were very concerned about my safety. After checking me into the hotel, they talked to the owner to verify that the gates to the entrance would be locked at night. They told me not to answer any knock on the door.

By this time it was very late. The woman receptionist and two girls came to my room and insisted on visiting. They wanted to know all about the United States and me. I was a curiosity to them. I had eaten very little all day, so I ordered a couple of beers to help gain a partial recovery. I asked to be awakened at 3:00 A.M. The room had only cold water, and a candle for light.

In the morning, I crawled out of bed and put on the same clothes by candlelight. It was pitch-black outside. There I was, walking the mile to the bus stop in the dark. At the stop, there were crude stalls set up with food and drink. People were milling all around. I don't remember eating anything. I grabbed a cup of coffee. A real "rattle-trap" arrived and we were off for the two hour ride into the ruins. We passed through virgin countryside. There was fog hovering over rugged mountains, garnished with a full moon. The bus driver played full blast tapes of Latin music from Mexico and Honduras.

We arrived at 7:30 A.M. at the Copân Ruins. I was dropped off at the main entrance, but they did not open until 8:00 A.M. A young girl helped me with my luggage, locking it in a room so that I could take the tour. This was a modern facility with maps, models, and guides.

In walked Napoleón. He came to take me on a two hour walk through the ruins. He told me everything as the two of us, all alone, wandered here and there. We climbed up and down and in and out and even went deep into two tombs, using a cigarette lighter. They were well preserved.

Just as the French general, Napoleón had a well-planned strategy and there were moments when I was a little on edge, but all went well. It was certainly worth the harrowing haul from Tegucigalpa.

After I returned to the United States, I corresponded with the two men I had hitchhiked with. One was a T.V. repairman and needed a tester. I sent one to him, but he never received it because it was stolen.

The same little "rattle-trap" bus appeared to take me to San Pedro Sula, farther to the north. This time it was loaded, but I did get a seat. As we progressed through mountainous countryside, they jammed more people in at every little town and at every shack we passed by. Eventually the bus was overflowing. We would stop at an occasional hut in the hills where two or three people would board. Finally, they started putting the passengers and their belongings up in the luggage racks on the roof. Legs, boots, and shoes were dangling down by the window on the side where I was seated. At one stop, someone ran up to the bus with a gorgeous red chicken with its legs tied. It was hoisted up to the rack on top along with the passenger. I started laughing and couldn't stop. Everyone was staring at me as if to say: "What's the matter with her?" This was an everyday, normal procedure for them. We arrived at one man's shack and he had to climb out of the window to get off the bus.

At one of these stops, a poignant scene unfolded. A very poor man was waving goodbye to his family who had just climbed up on the roof. I snapped a picture of the scene. The man waving had a terrible sadness in his eyes. I could tell he did not appreciate my filming. There he was standing forlorn, his humble shack in the background. This has tugged at my heart to this day. It is one picture I wish I hadn't taken.

We arrived at Entrada where the bus was just leaving for San Pedro Sula. We ran to catch it. We were jammed in again. There was no breakfast, no lunch. I was starving. One passenger was holding in his hand what looked like tamales. I asked him how much they had cost. He said ten. I thought he meant ten *lempiras*, so I said no I wouldn't buy any. As we took off, he handed me one of his tamales. I gulped it down. It was delicious corn masa with frijoles wrapped in banana leaves. I found out later he had paid *centavos*. I could have had ten for one lempira. Furthermore, I think I could have eaten ten.

We rode the very crowded bus for two hours. I visited non-stop with these friendly, lovable people. I pulled out a twenty dollar bill from my money belt and a man gave me sixty lempiras for it . . . a three to one exchange.

I climbed off the bus at San Pedro and headed for the airport to catch a plane to the island of Roatan. This is a scuba diving hangout. We landed very late and the night was closing in. I was met by

Santiago, the owner of the hotel, and his educated daughter. She tended to be extremely rude. I kept thinking I could hardly wait to get a nice room, a hot bath, a change of clothes, and a drink before a delicious dinner. These hopes were a paradise lost. A bridge had washed out during a heavy rainstorm, so we had to park the car by the side of the road and walk down a trail five or six blocks. I had to carry my bag down a steep slope along a path at the edge of the beach. I couldn't see, it was so dark. We walked and walked. I thought I would not make it.

Upon arriving, I found that there was no hot water, so I gave up, had a couple of stiff drinks, and sat down to dinner. It was certainly savory. We had home-cooking which consisted of roast pork, mashed potatoes and gravy. I retired early and slept well. However, in the night the electricity was cut off. I did not even have a candle. I couldn't find the toilet. I had reservations for another night, but this was too much. I packed and got ready to leave.

There were no hard feelings. Santiago, a black man, and I had an amiable conversation. I was given a large purple fan coral as a remembrance. It is exquisite. Even now it remains on display in my family room.

I was driven to the small airport and had to wait three hours before a plane came to take me to La Ceiba. Santiago came back to say goodbye again. He kissed my hand.

La Ceiba is a beautiful little city to the north, situated on the Caribbean. Its name comes from an Arawakan Indian word for the trees which flourish here. This is a West Indian and Mexican tree, *la ceiba,* which yields kapok. A cottony silky fiber, covering the seeds of these kapok trees, is used for mattresses, life preservers, and insulation material. Also, this was the headquarters of the Standard Fruit and Steamship Company. Bananas, coconuts, and rubber were exported.

I went to a lovely hotel with swimming pool and bar, where I met many people. A young girl attended the bar. One gentleman was from the Cayman Islands. Another man at the bar was staying in the hotel for Christmas Eve because he had so many relatives come to his house. I befriended a very old man who was the swimming instructor. I gave him a Christmas kiss and asked him to dinner, but he wouldn't join me. He agreed to let me buy him a chicken dinner to take home. I relished a delightful dinner of fish.

I must not forget to mention a small boy, sitting on the steps at the airport, when I arrived. He was dirty and barefoot. I asked him what he wanted from St. Nicholas. He said: "zapatos" (shoes). I asked him how much they would cost. He said:" ten, more or less". I gave him ten lempiras. He was radiant and dashed into the airport. At once, two other tiny boys dashed out and sat on the steps. I had to disappoint them.

The next morning, after walking around the plaza, I took a bus back to San Pedro Sula. The drive was scenic with mountains looming in the background. My luck had changed from the experience in Roatan.

Another first class hotel was waiting for me in San Pedro. The first thing I did was to look for a big hamburger. Sitting around the pool in the evening, I visited with three waitresses. We captured a rapturous rainbow holding up the sky with bedazzling chromatic colors. One precious waitress appeared carrying homemade tamales for me. We ate together.

In the morning, it was time to take a bus back to Tegucigalpa. All of the passengers were friendly and talkative, as usual. I visited at length with a young girl, Soraya. She gave me a cassette with the music of Honduras.

Upon arriving, I went immediately to relate my experiences to Luz, at the travel agency. She and I walked up a very steep road in the mountains surrounding Tegucigalpa. Up here, she took me to her house to meet her family which included her dear grandmother. We went back down into the city marketplace. Luz introduced me to green mangoes served with salt and pimiento. We had meat on skewers cooked on the outdoor grills. This was a delightful delicacy, even though we stood in the open-air market in the middle of the street.

I was booked on a flight to San Jose, Costa Rica. Off I went, arriving very late the next day. That evening, at the hotel, I encountered a group of very intoxicated Americans. I visited with their tour guide,

Sergio. As he held his hand to his head, we erupted into laughter at the thought of his having to accompany them for a week.

The first tour was to the Poas Volcano. Leaving San José, we passed through much rolling countryside of coffee plantations. We drove quite a distance to the foot of the volcano, where there was a museum. We climbed up a slope for a half a mile or more. Reaching the top, we looked down upon the crater. There was little to see. A dense fog was hanging over it. There was a combination of fog and steam with the strong odor of sulfur. The wait was almost an hour, but nothing seemed to be happening. At last, it appeared to be an impossible venture. We walked dejectedly back down to the museum. Then, miraculously, the sun broke through. Several of us raced back up the hill to see the volcano and take photos. Even though it wasn't that spectacular, there are always those two or three people who never give up.

I had been visiting with a young girl, Beatriz, from Medellín, Colombia. We had the guide drop us off in the city on our way back from Poas. We walked miles following a big parade. I don't remember what they were celebrating, but there were many interesting costumes. The typical Latin exuberance was displayed. We topped this off with a big Chinese dinner.

Next was a trip through mountains and rainforest on our way to Limón, on the Caribbean. After our investigation of the town, we ended up at an outdoor restaurant. As we were waiting to be seated, we noticed that several large tables near us were being decorated. There was a great deal of excitement. After inquiring, we were told that President Arias and his huge party were having lunch there. So we all had lunch together. He joined us to be photographed when we expressed our admiration for him. We were all very excited and he appreciated the attention.

One might wonder why we had so much respect for President Arias. Costa Rica is unique. It stands out not only as a leader in conservation but also for its rare biodiversity. It has had a stable solid democratic government for some time now. It is Latin America's oldest democracy and has the highest literacy rates. There is no army. It is seen as a stark contrast to its neighbor, Nicaragua and other Latin American countries. After the attack on Pearl Harbor, this small country declared war on Japan on December 8, 1941, before the United States did. Declarations against Germany and Italy followed on December 11th.

Our last tour was a lovely drive through the mountains to the Pacific Ocean by the old Spanish route of 1606. This is one of the most scenic roads in all of Costa Rica. We stopped for a delightful breakfast of chicken, sour cream, tortillas, beans and rice. We were on our way to Carara Biological Reserve and Jaco Beach. On our way, we saw an enormous salt water crocodile in the mouth of a river.

The rain forest of Carara covers a large mountainous area in a zone of transition from the dry north Costa Rican Pacific to the humid coast of the south. It could be called a dry rainforest, for in spite of the lush vegetation it has a sparse undergrowth. This makes it easier to observe the abundant wildlife.

The most easily seen are the macaws, parrots, parakeets, toucans, hummingbirds, flycatchers, kingfishers, and many birds of prey. The insect fauna consists of a spectacular array of butterflies, large beetles of metallic colors, centipedes, and wasps and bees. There is a variety of cats such as the jaguar, puma, jaguaroundi, and ocelot. They are not seen often. The howler monkey, the white-faced monkey, the spider monkey, and the squirrel monkey can be observed easily. During the day, deer, coatis, sloths, porcupines, coyotes, armadillos, and many others are active.

The diversity of the trees forming the high canopy is one of the greatest in the world. About sixty-one families of plants have been described. Many trees bloom in varied patterns of incredibly colorful flowers.

As we started into the forest on a trail, we were accosted by two men, who looked the part of bandits. The bus driver and guide were very nervous. They told us later that they had told these men we were on a pre-paid tour and no one was carrying money. The police were notified.

The rainforest lived up to its name. It started raining. We walked in quite far. Most of the hike was in the rain. We became soaking wet and very cold. My white slacks and white blouse were covered with mud. I feared I would lose my contacts. We tried to seek protection under banana leaves with little luck. We kept looking for macaws and calling to the monkeys. It was hilarious. One of the members of the tour was an extremely obese man in shorts with a beard and moustache. He kept calling out to the monkeys without a break. The monkeys loved him and answered him. Then we had an old typical Texan with his sweet little wife joining in. I am sure these conditions diminished our chances of viewing many animals and birds.

On our way back to San José, we stopped at a restaurant for snacks and hot brandy to warm our cold bodies.

The flight back to Tegucigalpa with the connection to the United States was uneventful. I was being carried away from my lovely dream world to harsh reality again. 1988 was gone! O.K! Where to next? As soon as possible!

Spring Break—Tela, Honduras

Back to Honduras in March of '89, I headed for the beaches of Tela, on the Caribbean. During the flight on the Honduran airplane, I admired the beautiful apron the azafata (stewardess) was wearing. She gave me the apron. It is a lovely white bib apron with magnificent embroidered flowers. I was overcome and thanked her profusely.

On arriving in Tegucigalpa, I was met by Luz and a small boy. She advised me on how to get to Tela.

Again, I found myself in the Hedman bus station. I had to buy my ticket at eight in the morning for the one o'clock afternoon bus. I waited and watched two or three full buses leave before I could get on. Then I realized that this one was also full. The driver escorted me all the way to the back to a shelf. I was so grateful just to get on. A team of volleyball players was on the bus. One of them gave me his seat. They were a lively group. Eating the entire time, they shared with me "los deditos." This is a pastry in the shape of a finger.

We got to San Pedro Sula. I grabbed a bus for El Progresso. The name on the bus was ironical. It was a very old antique, that barely functioned. It was jammed full. An elderly blind man sat with me. A young man in front stared at me constantly. I checked to see if all the buttons on my blouse were buttoned. We passed fincas (ranches) and fields of rice. I had to change buses in El Progresso.

In El Progresso, many children got on the bus, selling everything, including paper bags of chicken. They were all breasts. I asked for a leg. There were none, but a little boy said, with a twinkle in his eyes, "'Hay una pierna dentro." (there is a leg inside). I gave him a coin for his humour and sly salesmanship deceit, but did not take the chicken.

From El Progresso to Tela, the scenery was mountainous and gorgeous. In Tela, I found a young taxi driver with a broken-down car. He had to start it with a screwdriver and sparks were flying. The horn worked only by touching two wires together. I had to laugh, but did try to exercise control, so I wouldn't hurt his feelings.

He dropped me at the hotel on the beach. It was an enormous rustic complex. There were separate cottages along the beach. They put me in pretty blue and white one. The atmosphere was a combination of Brazil and Jamaica. Music played loudly all night, and the people were noisy. They never stopped talking.

All of this country near the ocean was populated long ago by the Mayas, coming from Copán and Yucatan. The inhabitants were the Xicaques Indians. Xicaques is a Mayan word meaning "linen of the forest." These people were descendants of the prehistoric Americans, fitting somewhere between the primitive man and contemporary man.

In the Bay of Tela, there was the village of Tehuacán. This Mayan word means "the place of the lions". Tehuacán was later called Triunfo de la Cruz (triumph of the cross) and finally Tela.

In 1498, Americo Vespucio, Italian navigator and geographer in the service of the Catholic king and queen, sailed along the coasts of this bay. In 1502, Columbus investigated this same area.

As in North America, the Indian population did not fare well. There were many conquests which brought suffering to the original inhabitants, the Indians. The governor of Cuba sent expeditions to capture many and transport them to Cuba as slaves.

From 1860 until his death in 1864, one man cared for the Indians. He was the Spanish missionary, Manuel de Jesús Subirana.

He founded the village of Jilantrique on the River Jilán. This is considered the first district (barrio) of Tela. Subirana established an indigenous community and constructed the first hermitage. He was an extraordinary man with a great love for humanity and a notable teacher, who learned easily the idioms and dialects of the Indians. He was responsible for teaching these people through religion. He also taught them the rudiments of agriculture in the cultivation of beans and corn. Platanos and bananas were first planted in Honduras by Father Subirana and his Indians. The community prospered, but in 1864 a fire destroyed Jilantrique, with its houses of straw and flammable material. The hermitage, made of adobe, was the only building saved. The superstitious Indians attributed this to a miracle.

The Indians had learned to hate the white conquerors for their cold-blooded oppression. Few had defended the Indian. Father Bartólome de las Casas, Spanish missionary and historian, is worthy of mention. He was called the "Apostle of the Indies." He crossed the ocean fourteen times to get on his knees before the Catholic king and queen, Isabella and Ferdinand, of Castilla and Leon. He begged them to recognize the plight of the American Indian and asked for clemency toward them. He also sought help in the conversion and the breaking of the power the Spanish landowners had. Finally, Queen Isabella arrived at the conclusion that the Indians were human and should be treated as such.

De las Casas went to the Indies with his father. They went to Hispaniola in 1502. Eight years later, he was ordained a priest. In 1514, he began the work to improve the conditions of the Indian, which included the abolition of Indian slavery, and the forced labor of the Encomienda. This was a commission or royal land grant which gave the conquistador complete control over the Indians and the land. It created terrible hardships.

De las Casas tried to establish an Indian colony, but was unsuccessful. He went to Peru with a royal *cedula* prohibiting Indian enslavement. He worked with the Indians in Guatemala for a while and was Bishop of Chiapas, Mexico. In a state of anxiety, he endorsed a plan to import Negro slaves, but repented at once. Through his humanitarian striving for the benefit of the Indians, new laws were adapted in 1542 to protect them, but very soon rendered impotent. His *Historia de las Indias* was published in 1875. We find valuable historical and anthropological material in his writings.

After this digression, I shall return to my stay in Tela. The first morning, I walked far up the beach. I passed several tents which housed snakes, eagles, and vultures. This was a private collection, which I filmed. I returned to sunbathe. There was fresh fish and lobster for lunch and dinner.

The next day, I waited for my taxi driver to take me to Lancetilla, an enormous botanical garden. We traveled on a terrible road, which used to be the tracks of the trains transporting bananas. There was a large variety of trees and plants in the garden. They came from many countries such as Asia, the Philippines, Brazil, and Polynesia. A collection of orchids and ornamental trees could be purchased. There were many birds in this habitat. I wandered about for some time, taking pictures.

On the way back, we stopped at a bridge over a river filled with huge rocks. The taxi driver lifted me down to the rocks to photograph. We made a date to go to Triunfo de la Cruz the following day.

Early in the morning, we set off again. After a short drive, we arrived in the original settlement of Tela founded by Father Subirana. It was extremely interesting, now made up of a typical black society.

There were numerous shacks on the beach, some of wood and some of adobe. Almost all had palm thatched roofs. Colorful clothes were hanging out to dry, everywhere. There were a few very nice new little wooden houses sprinkled here and there. All seemed to have chickens running around in their yards. The vendors were prolific. Restaurants lined the beach. I was reminded of Brazil. Many children were busy trying to sell something. It was picturesque.

The driver had dropped me off and said he would return for me. I sunbathed for a long time on a completely remote beach, then I wandered back to a restaurant and ordered "Sopa Marinera." There was a whole fish and crab in this delightful soup. It had a fantastic flavor, but caused me to work hard getting to the meat. I sat on a crude cane bench on the oceanfront. Many black children joined me with their items to sell. I visited at length with a beautiful little eight-year-old girl. She told me her mother had left to go to Boston eight years before and never returned. My heart ached.

The driver appeared to take me back to the hotel. When he dropped me off, he gave me an old book, first edition, on the history of Tela. It was moldy and wrapped in newspaper. I know it meant a lot to him. Tears came to my eyes. When I returned to the United States, I mailed a package to him filled with shoes, shirt, razor set, and a gold watch. Another hopeless attempt, he never got it.

The next two days I spent on the beach, walking a great distance along the oceanside, taking pictures of the Negroes selling goods. A few people went by on fast galloping horses. I went swimming with two men from Tegucigalpa and three girls with an inner tube. I took many pictures of everyone. They enjoyed this, posing for as many as I could shoot. I mailed copies back to everyone. It was time to take the bus back to Progresso, San Pedro, and Tegucigalpa.

The morning I was going to leave for the United States. I went down to the restaurant very early. Here everyone was eating and dancing in a frenzy. It had been going on all night. I danced with them for a short time and left hurriedly to catch the plane. Mechanical trouble put us into a hotel, where sandwiches were served. The wait was lengthy. A priest in a long white robe, wearing a beard, and carrying a heavy cross around his neck was waiting with us. A group of Mexican missionaries from Chihuahua, entertained us with two guitars, singing to the top of their voices.

It had to end. I got back home again with my head in the clouds for several days, but I soon came down with a jolt and finished the school year with renewed vigor.

Guanaja, Honduras—July 1989

I was off!! Guanaja is another little island just east of Roatan, in the Caribbean. I saw three of them on the map I bought in Honduras. The third is a very small one called Utila. They are called Islas de la Bahia (islands of the bay). They are quite close to the mainland.

I arrived here to find my accommodations were in a small modest hotel. The settlement was very small with the ocean all around. I met a young couple from Italy. We went everywhere together, even if there was no where to go but up and down the few streets that existed.

One day we rented a boat to take us to a remote beach. We sunbathed for several hours and investigated the flora. I found a huge beetle that I had to carry home with me. It was the size of a small mouse. It still sits on the bookcase in my family room. We were attacked by sand flies. It was their season. After being thoroughly bitten on every inch of exposed body area, we were quite relieved to see our boat coming back to pick us up.

After several days of this, I was ready to take a boat to Trujillo, on the mainland. The Italian couple was going with me. We made arrangements to leave one day, but the captain of the boat was on a drinking binge. He was unable to pilot his boat, and the trip was postponed until the next day. The Italian couple was afraid to go with him and cancelled. I climbed on the boat the next day by myself. It was a fun trip across the bay. We were served fried fish for lunch. Our captain had sobered up a little, but when we got to the wharf in Trujillo and tried to dock and tie up, he had a terrible time. He made several stabs at it. The people on the dock thought this was hilarious. We finally got fairly close, but there was still quite a gap between the boat and the wharf. I had to jump with plenty of help. I did not feel very comfortable..

An American was involved in part of the history of Trujillo, Honduras. It is a story almost beyond belief. William Walker (1824-1860) was born in Nashville, Tennessee. He had become a doctor, lawyer, and journalist by the time he was twenty-four years old. He had a hard time settling down. He is described as a one hundred pound, gray-eyed, tight-lipped, egocentric, puritanical ascetic who believed he had a certain destiny. He went to San Francisco in 1850 and in 1853 he invaded lower California, intending to capture this area and Sonora from Mexico. This was a failure. He was tried for violation of neutrality laws and was acquitted.

In June 1855, he and fifty-eight followers colonized Nicaragua. He outsmarted the existing liberals and conservatives and was elected President in July 1856.

He was confronted by an Alliance of Central American States, and pressure from Cornelius Vanderbilt, whose transit company controlled Walker's supply lines. Then came defeat and a surrender to the United States Navy in May, 1857.

There were many in the United States who supported Walker. President Pierce vacillated between Walker's Nicaraguan Government, with its possible admission to the Union as a slave state and the danger of alienating Great Britain who had an interest in Nicaragua. Britain's influence had been established on the east coast in the 17th century when San Juan del Norte was seized in 1848. Along this coast, there had been frequent raids by English and Dutch buccaneers.

Walker returned to the United States as a hero and was acquitted again. From the Bay Islands of Honduras, he made a final attempt in 1860 to conquer Central America declaring himself President of Nicaragua. Trujillo was captured and held briefly by Walker in this same year, however, he was forced to surrender to the British Navy and was turned over to Honduras. This famous filibuster was shot by a firing squad in Trujillo in September, 1860.

I stayed several days in a small hotel which seemed more like an inn. I became friends with the owner and her daughter. I was driven all around the area and hung out in markets, museums and antique stores. Most of my time was spent recuperating from the sand flies of Guanaja and washing my clothes. Every inch of my body had been bitten by these flies. I was miserable for several days with the itching. I did find time to garden in the large planter on the verandah of my hotel room. I weeded and dug around in the soil. It was comforting to my tormented body to get back to the earth.

I returned to Tegucigalpa by bus. Since the flies had chased me away from Guanaja, I ended up with a few extra days. I took a bus for La Esperanza to the west. This was a very small village. There was nothing to do but wander through the open air markets. I had taken this side-trip, primarily, to view the countryside. It was beautiful.

I met a young girl who was staying at the hotel. She was with the Peace Corps, involved with the civil war problems in Salvador. She worked very near the border of Salvador and Honduras. I gathered that it was a rather dangerous assignment.

Next was a day trip from Tegucigalpa to Valle de Angeles. I had been told it was a picturesque village, *precioso*. I had a problem on the way. We were stopped halfway there and asked to produce our passports. I had left mine in the hotel room. I pleaded with the official to let me get back on the bus. He was persistent. He said I could go no further. I stood by the side of the road and started crying. Eventually, another bus came by and he allowed me to go on my way to the village. My spirits were dampened. It really turned out to be not worth the hassle.

¿POR QUÉ?
(*Inspired while strolling the streets in Tegucigalpa, Honduras*)

Solamente las montanas perseveran.
Los humanos frágiles perecen
Con sus angustias
Con sus soledades y sufrimientos.

Los olvidados en la calle
Cruzando pidiendo
Pidiendo cruzando
Hombros curvados
Como un "'question mark."
¿Por qué?

I took a few unusual photographs, but my heart wasn't in it.
It was time to go back to the United States, while I was still even.

Galapagos Islands—Machu Picchu
December 1989

Being a Biology and Earth Science teacher, I had dreamed about going to the Galapagos Islands for many years. When we got to the section in our thick heavy Biology book on Darwin and his finches, I was enthralled—completely captivated. Even the geology fascinated me, with all of the volcanism, which is a study in itself.

I left Miami on December 16th to fly to Quito, Ecuador, South America's oldest colonial capital. Arriving in the evening, I found myself in the Chalet Suisse, a charming hotel. I shall always remember this hotel for its toilet, which made absolutely no noise when flushed. It was amazing. As I recall, it was made in Switzerland. I have often wondered why the United States could not produce a toilet like this. But then Archie Bunker would not have brought on so many of his laughs with one of this nature.

On the agenda the following day, was a full day excursion with a private car and driver. We drove seventy-five miles through the Avenue of Volcanoes. This is a valley flanked by snow-capped volcanic cones. Many sheep and cattle were browsing in the surrounding fields. We were on our way to the Indian Market at Pujilí.

The market was a typical outdoor market. This was an authentic one with no tourist hand crafts for sale. The Indians were dressed in their everyday garb, some wrapped in shawls and others in blankets. The women had babies strapped on their backs. Everyone wore hats, men and women. I saw several enormous stacks of huge cabbages on the sidewalk. I photographed a picturesque vendor wrapped in a turquoise blanket, wearing a dark hat. She was seated on the sidewalk surrounded by large stacks of onions, chiles, carrots, limes, and lovely red tomatoes. Several baskets were by her side filled with the overflow of produce. Large black pots were grouped on a stairway. This was an extremely colorful sight. There were numerous others just like her.

There was a butcher, with his meat hanging in front of his stand. Other pieces of meat lay out on the table in front of him. He was busy cutting off chunks of meat for two customers. They too, wore hats. Various kinds of food were being prepared on the grills set up here and there among the stalls.

I captured with my camera several most unusual sights. A large group of enormous pigs and hogs were coming down the middle of the street, like a stampede. My first impulse was to run for my life. Donkeys and llamas were appearing everywhere. Some were tied to a post near a store.

The variety of brilliant colors and textures, forming intricate patterns of objects, people, and movement, provided scenes for an impressionistic painting. As I write now, I am reviewing my photos and can hardly wait to take up my brushes.

On our way back to Quito, we stopped at an authentic colonial hacienda for lunch. I was impressed by the lane leading to the dwelling. It was lined solidly with huge majestic trees on both sides. We passed under this canopy for some distance to arrive at the house.

Then they gave me a day of "leisure." This is so typical of tour companies. It is amusing. This is one day they don't have to put out any tour money. I walked all over Quito for miles. I visited at length with everyone I ran into and could persuade to talk to me. There I was in the oldest colonial capital in South America. I took pictures of every colonial edifice I could find. Most were magnificent.

We were up early the next morning to catch a plane for Guayaquil. Here we had to board another plane for Baltra Island in the Galapagos, six hundred miles off the coast of Ecuador.

Not only is the airport situated on the Isla Baltra, but the Ecuadorean Navy and Air Force are based here. We went through an entry-type customs. It was more of a checking-in type procedure. Ecuador is very cautious and protective of these islands, only allowing a certain number of visitors in at one time. It is trying to protect the natural habitat and the plants and animals from being disturbed.

Here, we boarded our antiquated ship, the M/N *Bucanero*. I was told this was its last trip. Before starting our five days of island hopping, we strolled on the beach and observed some blue-footed boobies. I photographed one perched on the edge of a jagged rock jutting out over the water. He was elegant, despite his ridiculous name. His pale blue feet on the jet black rock, white head and breasts and black wings were lovely.

As we headed out to sea, we passed many unusual igneous formations. Some had been weathered by the lashing of the water into surrealistic patterns. There were sea lions lounging on some beaches. On others, the huge Galapagos turtles were crawling, sunbathing, or swimming in the water.

Each day we would stop at a particular island. We went off in small boats, to the edge of each one made up entirely of volcanic rocks, some being massive pure lava flows in fascinating patterns. Most had no sophisticated docking area. It was tricky getting off, jumping to steps or a ledge from the small boat. This was slippery business on the wet lava.

Darwin was amazed at the number of craters on these ten principal islands and guessed that there must be two thousand craters. Some were rising to a height of three to four thousand feet. Here on the islands, one finds either lava and scoria or finely stratified sandstone like tuff, which is a fragmentary volcanic rock composed of fine sands to coarse gravel.

Scoria, an ejected volcanic rock or extrusive, is vesicular. This means it is filled with "bubble holes." These are gas cavities (vesicles), formed by the release or escape of water vapor or gases after its ejection from a volcano. He also noted that all the craters examined had their southern sides much lower and broken down. He assumed that the craters had been formed while standing in the sea. Waves from the Pacific and trade winds had broken down the soft tuff.

In spite of being near the equator, the islands are not excessively hot, which might be because of the water brought here by the southern Polar current. Also, there is very little rain. The lower parts of the islands are lacking vegetation, but at a thousand feet or more you got more luxuriant vegetation. I was surprised at the starkness on first approaching the islands, some barren and foreboding.

Isla Bartolomé is where we found Bahia Sullivan. A tremendous igneous needle jutted up into the air on the edge of the water. We climbed to the top of a high hill overlooking the beautiful bay and numerous strange lava formations. There was magnificent vegetation the higher we went.

This was our first close encounter with the huge black sluggish aquatic lizards. They were sunning themselves on the jumbled black igneous rocks near the water. They resemble miniature alligators. Some are up to four feet long and may weigh twenty pounds. They live exclusively on the rocky sea beaches. Darwin states he had never seen one even ten yards in shore. They have strong claws and legs which help them crawl over the jagged and fissured masses of lava. Darwin opened the stomachs of several of these ugly creatures and found only seaweed which grows in thin green or dull red layers. He believed it grew in the bottom of the sea since he never did encounter any on the tidal rocks. These hideous reptiles are excellent swimmers. Their tails are flattened sideways and all four feet webbed. Darwin noticed that when frightened, the iguana will not enter the water. He threw one from the edge of the rocks into a deep pool. The iguana swam near the bottom gracefully and rapidly toward the shore. Near the rocks, it would conceal itself in seaweed or a crevice, then would crawl out on the rocks exactly where he had been thrown in. This experiment was repeated numerous times with the same results. Darwin surmised that this reptile had no enemy on shore, but could fall prey to creatures in the water such as sharks. Perhaps an inherited instinct forced it to seek the shore as a place of safety.

One of the sailors with Darwin sank one of these reptiles with a heavy weight, thinking it would die. After an hour, when his drew up the line he found the creature very much alive.

On the Isla Rábida (Jervis), the beaches were covered with sea lions. Enormous bulls would rear up among a whole pile of females and little ones. As we walked through the bushes, we would encounter a big bull partially hidden in among the growth. The vegetation consisted of many prickly pear and *palo santo*. We also saw pink flamingoes there.

I had worn my snorkeling leotard for several days and tried to get in the water at a beautiful spot where we had hiked. I couldn't take the cold water, so I never got completely in.

Islas Santa Cruz has thirty-five hundred inhabitants. We found many restaurants, bars, and souvenir shops. This is where the Charles Darwin Research Station is located.

The most spectacular sight was the great number of giant Galapagos tortoises. I have a photo of seven of these giants all together. I have pictures of myself and the guide holding up the head of one. Their size was unbelievable. One of our group even has his arm around the neck of one as if he were caressing it.

There were also numerous sea lions lying on the black lava. I captured one scene where a tiny yellow breasted bird was standing on the rocks among the sprawling sea lions.

On Islas Plazas there are more colonies of sea lions lounging everywhere on the black igneous rocks. After our small boats let us off on each island, we wandered all around. Another little yellow bird stood so still against the harsh black backdrop. He posed for me. He looked so delicate.

Hundreds of large bright red crabs crawled over the rocks near the water. Water and foam from the sea lapped up at the base constantly. These creatures produced a startling contrast to the dark matter on which they were moving.

We passed across one flat area that had reddish lichen-looking growth. Scattered among it were numerous cacti which resembled prickly pear, but the pads were clustered on top of a thick trunk.

We walked near the water's edge where the ocean was crashing up onto huge boulders with the foam swirling. It was a rugged scene. We observed more marine lizards and land lizards. The terrestrial variety differ slightly from their marine brothers. They are yellowish-orange beneath and a brownish-red color on top. They are just as ugly and appear stupid. They seem to be smaller. The movements of these creatures are of a lazy and torpid nature, slowly crawling along with their stomachs and tails dragging along the ground. They stop often to doze off for a short time with their eyes closed. They live in burrows which they have made in fragments of lava or in soft sandstone tuff. Darwin goes into great detail describing these reptiles. If disturbed, they curl up their tails, raising up on the front legs, nod their heads quickly and try to look fierce. They are not, however, and if they are tormented with a stick, they will try to bite it. Also, if two are held together on the ground, they will fight and bite each other until each loses blood over the matter.

Both of these lizards are herbivorous, even though the kind of vegetation each feeds on differs. The aquatic species is the only lizard that lives on vegetation from the ocean. The land variety consumes the succulent cactus. When the stomachs of some were opened, vegetable fibers and even the leaves of trees were found, especially of the acacia. Darwin broke off pieces of cactus and threw them to the lizards. It amused him to watch them seize the these pieces and carry them away in their mouths like a dog with a bone. They don't chew their food. Darwin notes that the little birds know that these creatures are perfectly harmless. He observed a thick-billed finch picking away at one end of a piece of cactus while a lizard ate at the other end. Then the little bird hopped up on the back of the reptile.

Isla Isabela (Albemarle) is covered with immense overwhelming amounts of black lava. This lava, which has flowed over the rims of caldrons as an overflow from a pot of boiling liquid, has spread over much of the seacoast. There are many cinder cones. Eruptions are known to have taken place there.

On the coast we saw more of the aquatic lizard, big and black. Inland we found the land variety. There are penguins there, but I did not see any.

We hiked up quite a distance to overlook the bay below where our ship was anchored, as Darwin's H.M.S. *Beagle* had been in 1835. We looked down on a lovely salt lake crater.

Isla Fernandina (Narborough), like Isabela, is covered with the black slag lava, resembling the slag from the mining of copper. In some places, it was gnarled and rope-like. Many cacti were growing against a background of leafless web-like vegetation. We found one type of short cactus with clustered arms of green. The tips of these arms were an orange color. They were growing in the crevices of lava. To me, this was an amazing feat. Sea lions and waterfowl, such as the blue-footed boobie, were at the water's edge. We witnessed a fight between two large lizards.

The guide led us to a tremendous lava armchair, complete with back and arm rests. It was called Neptune's Throne. I have a priceless picture of each of us sitting on this natural throne.

We walked by fantastic formations. One was a cavern where a torrent of water was rushing through. All around the precipitous edges, where the sea water was entering, numerous bright red crabs were crawling. The lava formations were so gnarled and violent with all kinds of irregular lines overhanging the swirling water below. One of these crabs was perched high on a ledge looking over the churning water. The pictures I took at this location were truly incredible, almost surrealistic.

Isla Santiago (James) is the home of many Galapagos hawks. We saw them soaring above and landing on the branches of the vegetation scattered among the unusual rock formations. They were not fearful and sometimes seemed to be posing. This is truly the island of birds. There are lava herons, Darwin finches, oyster catchers, yellow warblers, and the perpetual presence of the blue-footed boobie.

The oyster catcher caught my attention and my heart. It was a colorful bird with black and white plumage and a long red beak, which enabled him to procure small mollusks, for this is his diet.

Later, while on the ship, we passed a group of small penguins perched on a large rock at the entrance to an enormous cavern, probably carved out by the sea. We stopped again at Bartolome for another close encounter with groups of small sea lions lying on the beach. I was sitting among them, holding my hand out. They responded just as a puppy would. There was also a lovely lake with pink flamingoes.

One poignant memory, which remains vividly with me today, is Christmas Eve on the boat. A woman and her baby were on the boat. On this night, to the complete surprise of all the passengers, a small boat pulled up to ours. There came on board Joseph, Mary, with the baby Jesus, and the wise men. The crew members had put on costumes to portray and enact this Nativity scene. It was very emotional and appreciated by all of us. It is an indelible Christmas Eve experience.

We had to leave these magical islands and fly back to Quito the day after Christmas, Next on the agenda was a flight from Quito to Lima, Peru. We arrived in Lima at ten o'clock at night. I didn't intend to investigate this town. I met a middle-aged American couple who had stepped out of their hotel to walk around. The next time the man looked to see what time it was, he found his watch was gone.

We had to leave very early in the morning to fly to Cuzco (10,909 feet). At one time, this city was the capital of the Incan Empire. I found another source saying the elevation is 11,207 feet. It was occupied by pre-Incan tribes. Legend says it was founded by Manco Capac, the first Incan ruler. Its temples were filled with gold and silver. The Temple of the Sun, now in ruins, was at one time an important ceremonial place. It was supposed to have had walls covered in 700 sheets of gold. All was plundered by Pizarro in the 1530's. The colonial city used the ancient walls as foundations.

The first thing we noticed, upon arriving, was the effect of the altitude on your body. At the hotel, we were immediately served a tea made from the leaves of the coca shrub, in other words, cocaine. This was commonly prescribed.

The hotel was excellent. Just outside, the llamas wandered up and down the narrow streets. They were everywhere. Some Indians, dressed in their typical colorful garments, were leading their own pet llamas along the streets confronting the tourists. They asked to be photographed, but for a price. I did not participate in this business. I found it disgusting, so my album is lacking this unusual scene. I did some wandering around the city, but would not dare put my foot outside the hotel after the sun had gone down. I had been warned that there had been many robberies in the streets. Some tourists had even had a purse or backpack cut off as they walked along. I ran out of film and had to walk to the next corner to buy it. I asked a gentleman employee of the hotel to walk me there.

Next, was the spectacular bus trip through the Urubamba Gorge to the hotel at the entrance of the Machu Picchu ruins. Machu Picchu was discovered by the American explorer, Hiram Bingham in 1911. He thought he had found Vilcabamba, a stronghold where the Incas had fled to get away from the conquistadors. Spanish stories tell of the destruction of Vilcabamba in 1572. Now it is believed that a remote ruin in the Amazon is the lost city of Vilcabamba. It is not known whether the Incas occupied Machu Picchu before descending into Cuzco, or if they fled from the Spanish to this location.

I decided to do my exploring of the fabulous ruin early the next morning before our train left to return to Cuzco. I got up so early that the hotel was not even serving breakfast. I remember going back to the kitchen and grabbing what I could . . . rolls and coffee. It was very cold. I was wrapped up in my *ruana*, a type of shawl made in Argentina. This same ruana had served as my blanket on the boat. I headed for the ruins all alone. As I passed by the gatekeeper, he asked me where I was going. I informed him that I was going to take a particular hike. He said that I wouldn't be able to, as it was difficult, I shed my ruana, handed it to him, and said: "Keep this until I get back." I went along, like a turtle, at my own pace.

Part of the hike consisted of a series of stairs. I finally arrived at the end, a huge boulder, where everyone was sitting. Only a few had actually come up there, but they were from all parts of the world. Coming back down, I got some spectacular photos of the ruins, its walls and terraces. Huge clouds and mist moved in and hung among the pinnacles and peaks. In spite of this, I filmed the Urubamba River from a great elevation.

Returning from the hike, I wandered through all the ruins. I met an enthusiastic guide who was anxious to show me everything without charge. We spent some time together. We took pictures of each other perched on ancient walls or sitting on the sills of the rectangular windows of these walls. To me, the construction of all of these standing ruins with their windows, precisely measured, was excellent. It wouldn't take much to make this place quite livable. What a view! At times, the mist rolling in did create the impression and sensation of a dream world.

It was time to take the train back to Cuzco. The next morning I flew back to Lima and lounged around the hotel until my late pick up for the airport that night. I was back in Miami on January 1, 1990.

The Year of the Vera Cruz—1990

By this time, I was wracking my brain about where to go next for spring break. The name Vera Cruz, Mexico enchanted me. I decided to fly to Laredo, Texas, cross the border, and grab a bus or train for this city on the Gulf of Mexico. I did not have a schedule of trains or buses, but I thought it would be exciting to just arrive and take off on whatever was available and leaving at the moment.

The plane landed in Laredo at a very small and remote airport. There were no taxis waiting there. I had to go to a crossroads of sorts nearby, and wait for one. When a taxi arrived, I told the driver my plan. He took me across the border directly to a bus station. There was a bus leaving soon. I was lucky.

We rode along on the bus, on and on. It turned out to be a fourteen-hour ride to Vera Cruz. This was a very long ride for the few days I had. I began to realize that most of this trip was going to be on the bus, getting to my destination, and getting back to the airport in Laredo. This wouldn't give me much time to get a suntan on the beach.

There was one young Mexican man on the bus whom I shall always remember. At one of the rest stops, all of the passengers got off to buy refreshments. I must have been a little low on money. When this man got back on the bus, he had a Coke. I asked him how much it had cost. He told me 800 pesos. I shook my head "no" and told him that was too much money. I guess the 800 number frightened me. It turned out to be about a dollar. He left the bus again, returned, and handed me a Coke. I thanked him profusely. I felt embarrassed about making such a big deal about the money. We finally arrived in Vera Cruz with the typical bus fatigue syndrome.

After inquiring, I found an inexpensive hotel right on the water. On the waterfront, boats of many colors were tied up everywhere along the shore. Several large boats were docked at the piers extending farther out into the deeper water.

Vera Cruz is the most important port in this republic, competing with Tampico. In 1519, Cortes landed near the site which was later chosen to establish the present city. The surrounding area is a low sandy plain with many dunes and swamps. The land has been reclaimed and is very fertile. At one time, it was an easy prey to buccaneers during the 17th and 18th centuries. The harbor was guarded by the fortress of San Juan do Ulua. Its construction was begun in the 17th century. It was the last stronghold of the Spanish before their expulsion in 1821. In 1838 it was blockaded by the French, who were trying to collect for the damages suffered by French nationals. While fighting against the French landing, General Santa Anna lost a leg. The claims were taken care of. The French were out for a conquest. The adventure of Maximilian began.

The Austrian archduke, Ferdinand Maximilian (1832-1867), was denied a share in the imperial government by his brother, Franz Joseph. The Mexican conservatives asked for aid from Napoleon III to form an empire. Maximilian was persuaded to become emperor of this empire. He and his wife, Carlotta, left his palace in Trieste and sailed, in 1864, for Mexico. He had a problem from the beginning. He did not understand the Mexicans. Most of the country was loyal to Benito Juárez, the liberal Mexican statesman, who was a lawyer and a national hero.

Maximilian alienated the conservatives by his liberalism, and others by his 1865 decree ordering the execution of all followers of Juárez. His French soldiers drove Juárez to the north. He had no support from European monarchs. The United States had a civil war going on and was not friendly toward him.

Napoleon III withdrew the French soldiers in 1866-1867. The weak inadequate empire collapsed. The Empress Carlotta returned to Europe asking for help from Napoleon III and the pope. Maximilian considered abdicating, but decided to resist. After a siege by those opposing him in 1867, he was captured and shot.

Benito Juárez (1806-1872) was not only a statesman, but a lawyer involved in a political reform. He played an important role in this grim drama. He became governor of Oaxaca, Mexico. In 1853, he was imprisoned for opposing Santa Ana. After an exile in the United States, he was a figure in the Mexican Revolution. He became minister of justice and issued laws that attacked the privilege of church and army. At one time he was acting president, but was forced to flee with his government to Guanajuato, Guadalajara, and finally to Vera Cruz. He spent years in Vera Cruz during the War of the Reform.

I passed by a large metal plaque at Fort Ulua and prison honoring Juárez. It had been put there by the National Commission and the Institute of Mexican Youth, commemorating one hundred years since his death. Also, remembering the imprisonment he suffered in Vera Cruz in 1853, as a victim of despotism. It honors him as the defender of his country and for his belief that liberty and respect as a guarantee for the individual is the base for public peace. It is dated the tenth of April, 1972.

In 1914, there was a climax in the problems between Woodrow Wilson and Victoriano Huerta. United States sailors were arrested in Tampico. U.S. Forces landed in Vera Cruz and there was a brief battle. They surrounded and besieged the custom house for some time. Mexico broke off diplomatic relations.

I headed for the beach to work on a suntan. Several friendly Mexicans joined me. We had lively conversations. Another day, I wandered through the city to film many beautiful buildings and huge impressive nationalistic sculptures. Then I went on a complete tour of the fort and prison. I was my own guide, but always found someone to answer my questions.

There was a wall all along the beach. Men passed by on the streets nearby carrying large baskets filled with cooked shrimp. I bought large portions and carried them to my room to eat. Then, one day I purchased a very large portion, grabbed a cold beer from across the street, and went back to the wall. I climbed up on it and sat there watching the ocean, stuffing myself on the delectable shrimp.

I had to investigate the main mercado. It was typical, where one could see and purchase everything imaginable. I searched for my goat meat, I was successful. I went back to my hotel room to savor it.

It was inevitable. I had to climb back on that bus for the long ride to Laredo. I did find a charming hotel upon arriving. It was not impressive from the outside, but the inside was furnished with an array of Mexican tiles. There were numerous settings of Mexican handmade furniture, a fountain, and potted plants placed profusely about. The interior architecture was charming, with numerous stairways to interior balconies supported by structures at various angles. I didn't want to leave.

The morning of departure, I found a taxi driver to take me across the border to the airport in Laredo. We had a major problem and delay as I tried to cross. The border patrol took me into custody and held my passport. They said that I had failed to get a visitors pass when I entered the week before. It was true. My driver had taken me across and directly to the bus station. I was not given this paper. I did not even remember being stopped and offered this document, which now seemed to be the cause of a very serious violation. I was shocked, and explained the situation to the Mexican officials. They were cold and calculating, completely without emotion. The precious taxi driver insisted on waiting for me even as the time passed by. They refused to give me my passport, though I pleaded with them, citing the inconvenience for the taxi driver. I explained that he had three small children, and was losing other customers. All of this was to no avail. I knew what they wanted. They expected me to slip them some money, "the mordida" or bite as it is called. I told them I did not have money to give them, as I had only enough to pay the taxi driver and get home. In desperation and disgust, I asked, "Why don't you put me in jail?" I felt contemptuous and dared them. They didn't take me up on this proposal. I guess they thought I would give up after awhile. I kept asking for my passport. They were rough characters, who wished to demonstrate their pitiful authority and importance.

I started weeping. They showed no emotion. In fact, I was put in a small room by myself. Finally, after more than an hour, they gave me my passport and told me I could go. My faithful taxi driver was still waiting. I paid him all I could spare, leaving me just enough to get home.

MAPS

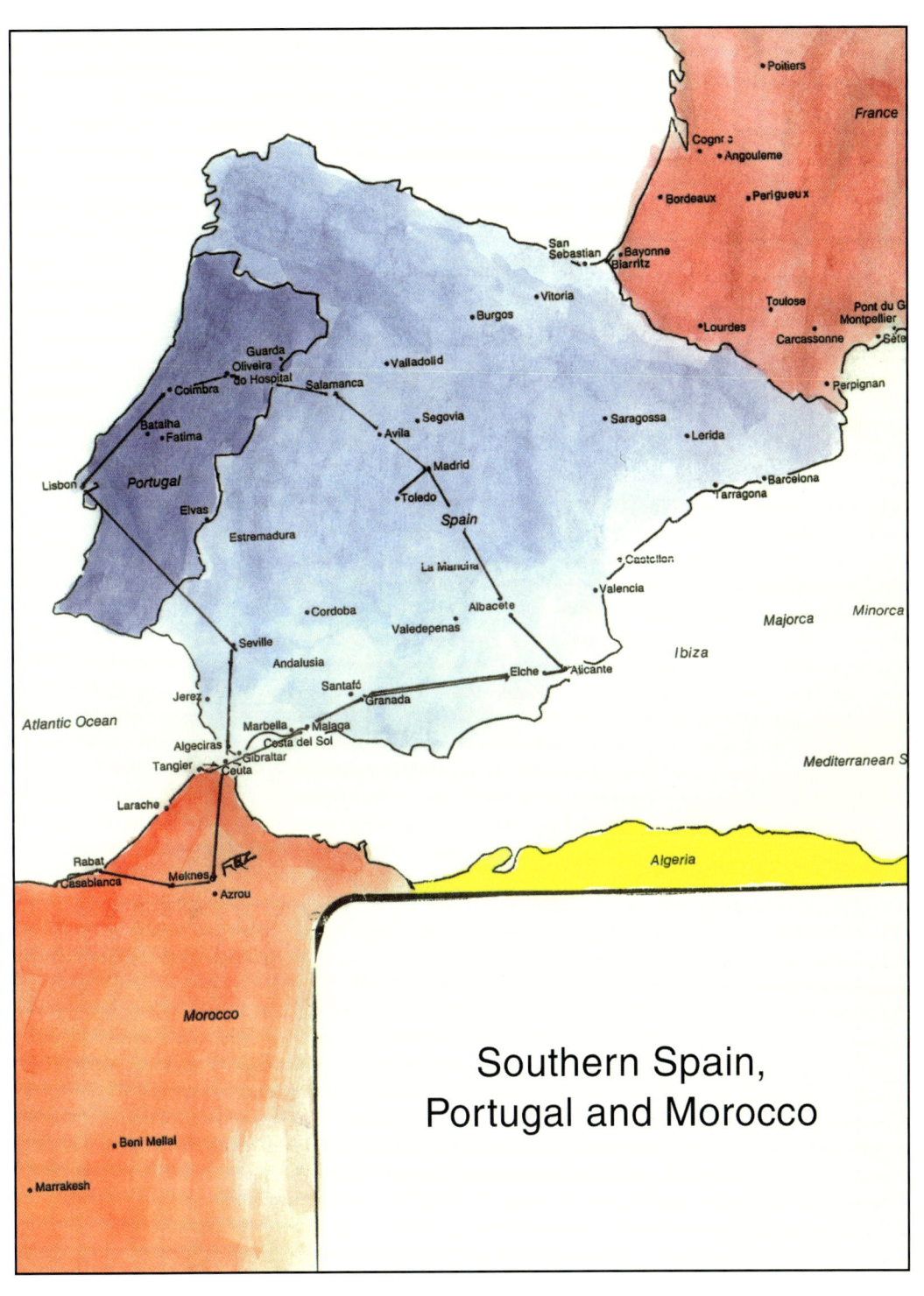

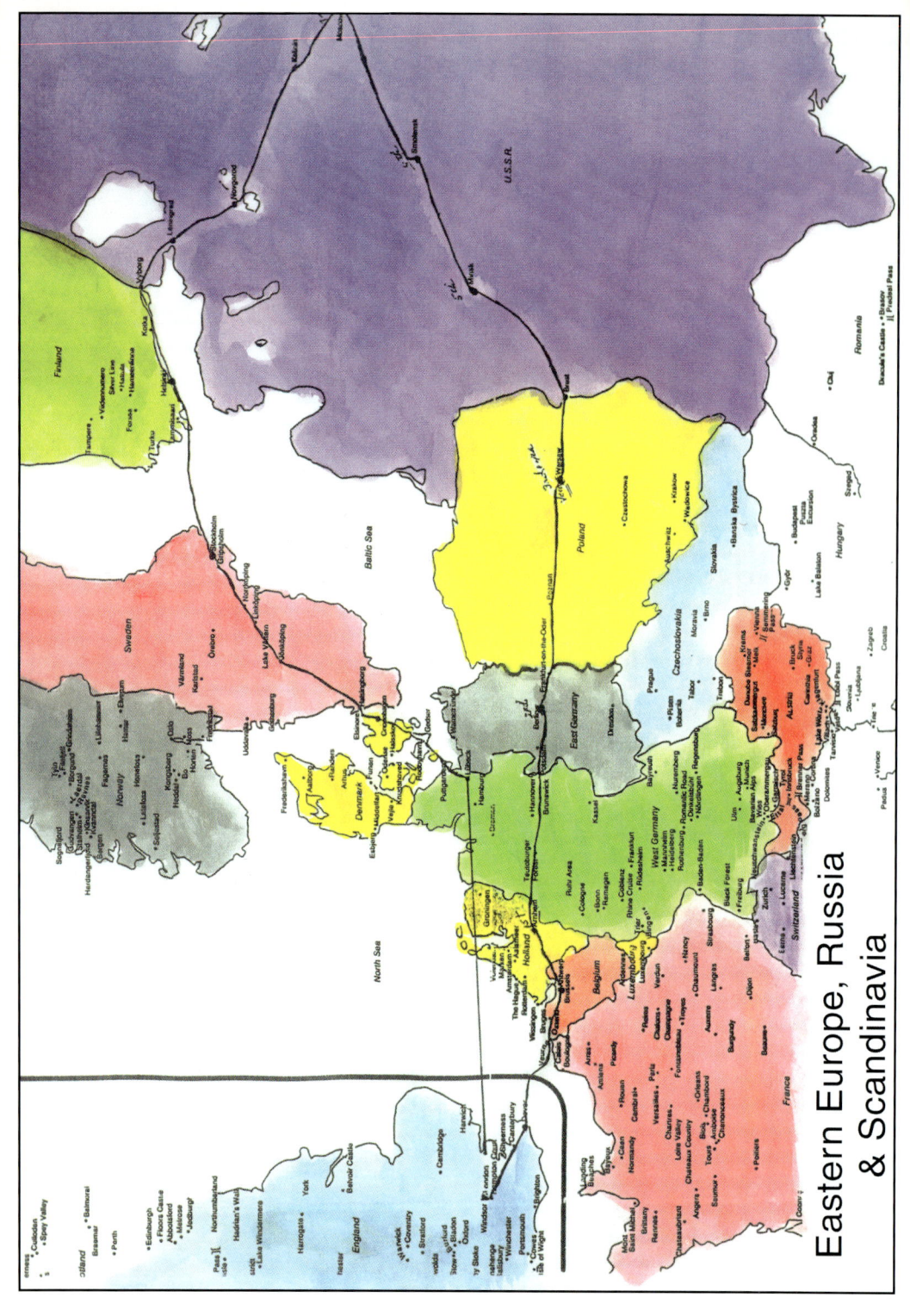

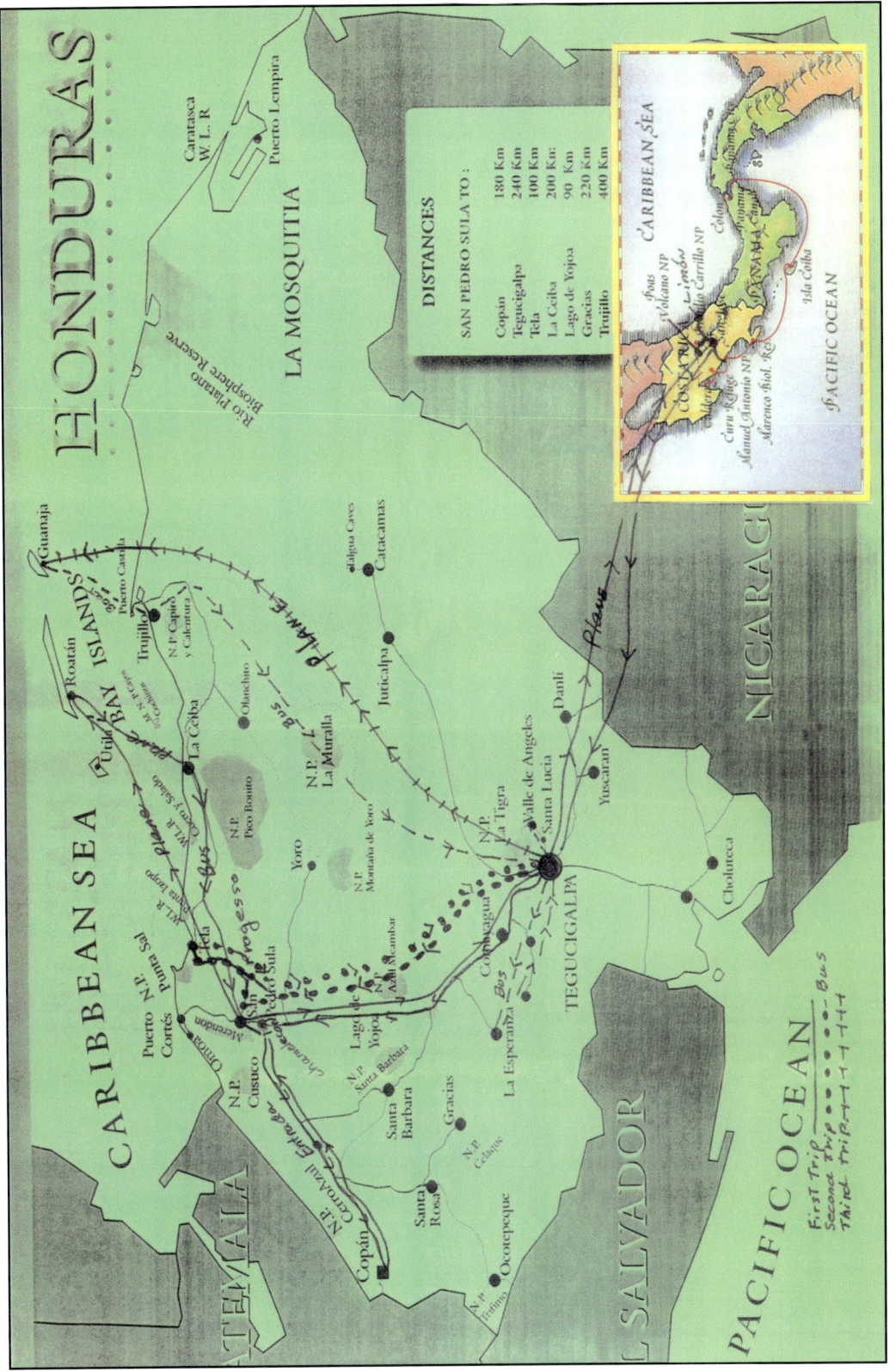

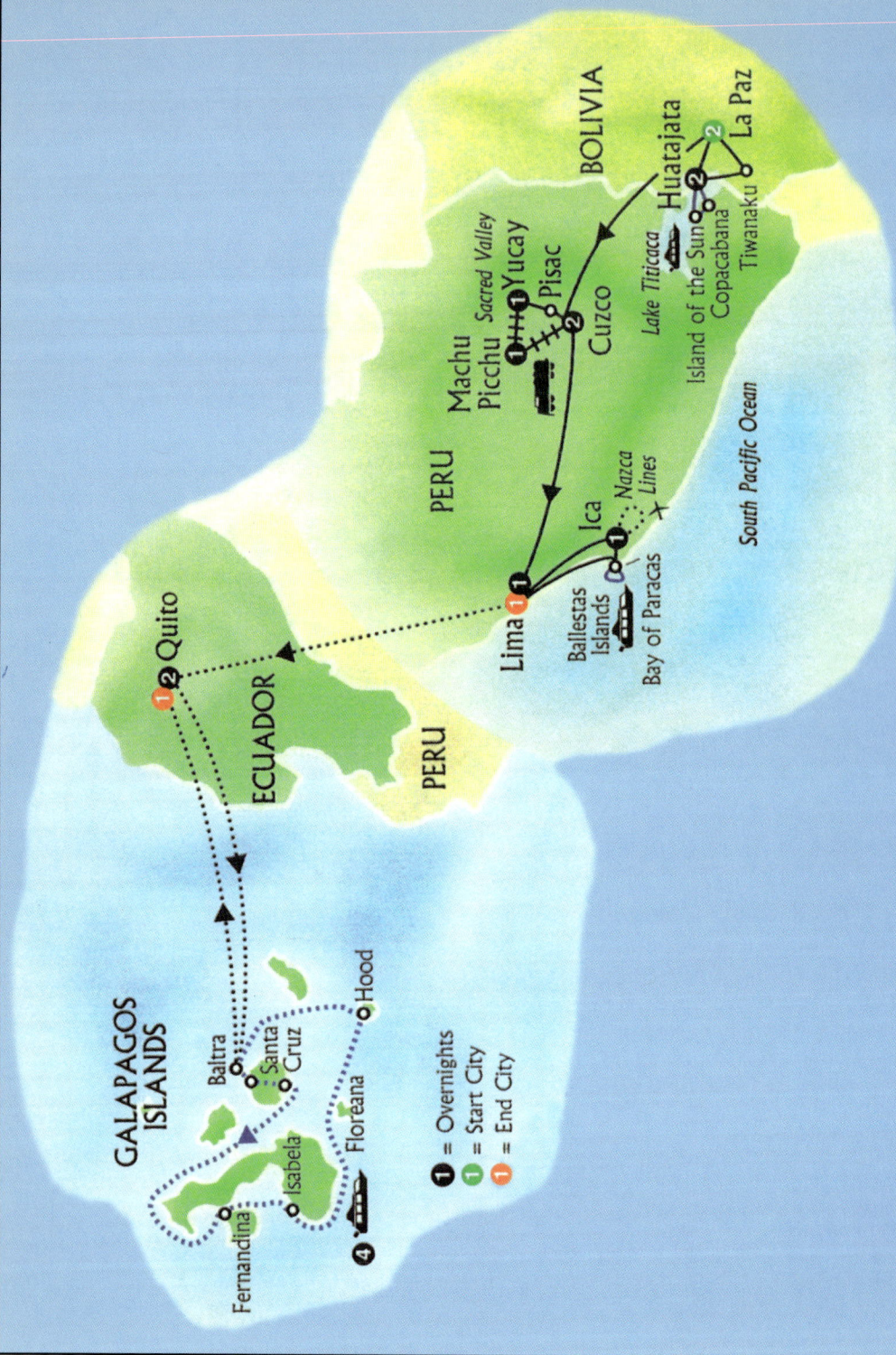

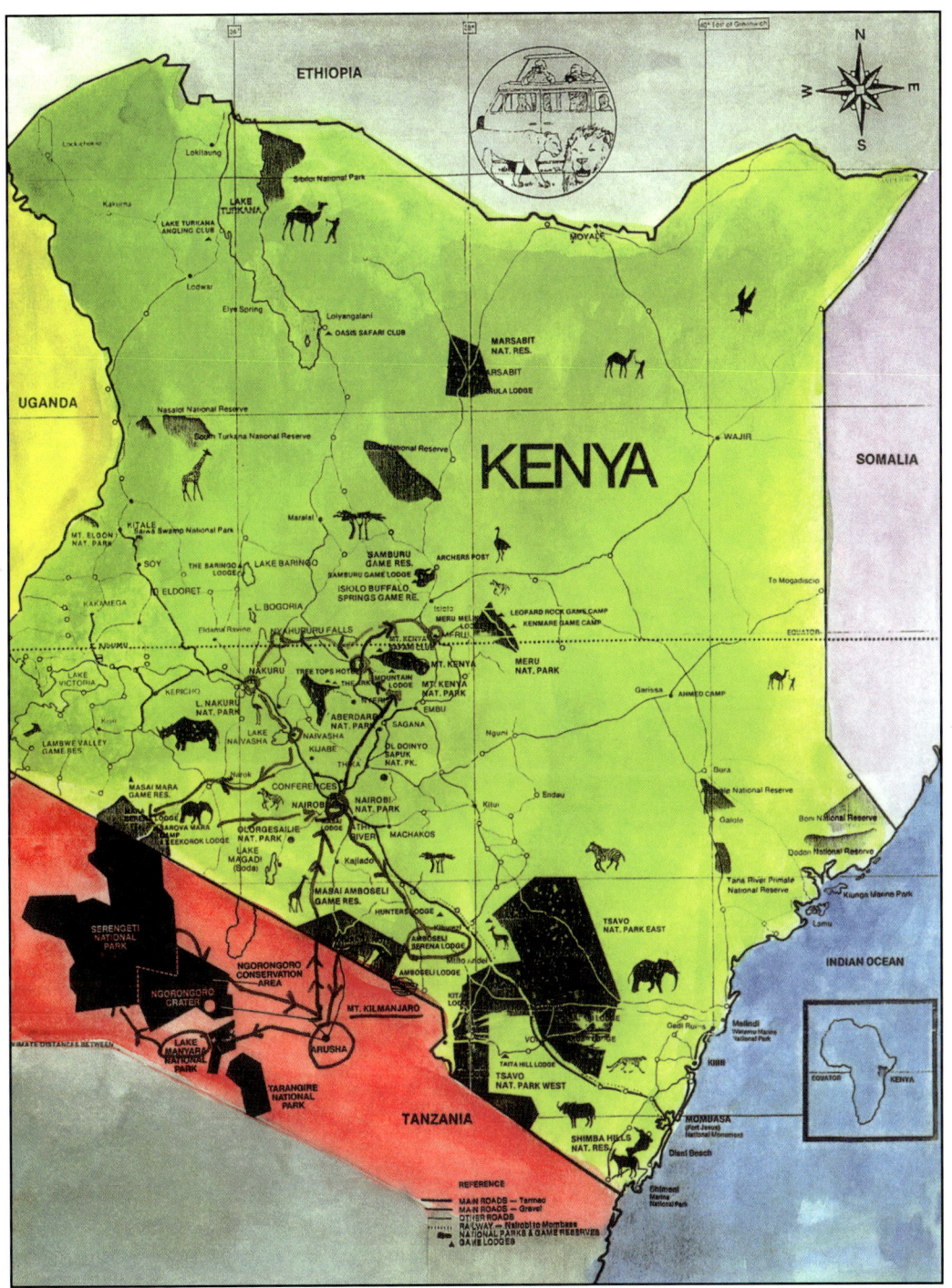

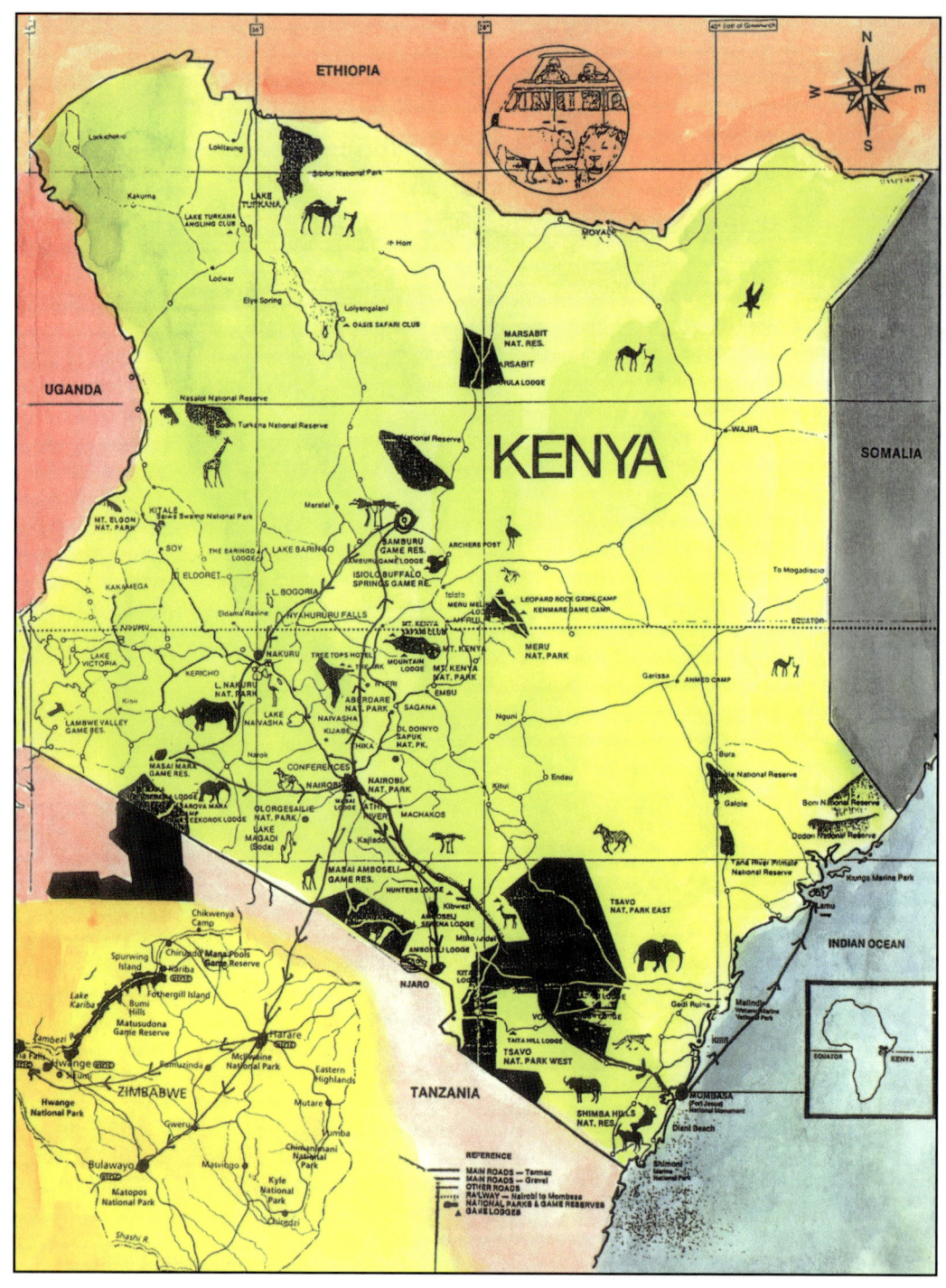

Vera Cruz—Summer 1990

I don't know why, but I decided to go back to Vera Cruz, even after my dreadful experience at the border in Laredo. This time I would fly to Mexico City and take another plane to Vera Cruz.

After arriving, I boarded a bus as soon as I could for Tapachula, Chiapas. This is about the farthest south you can get in Mexico. I wanted to look up the family of a young man I had met on the beach in Vera Cruz on my first visit. I have to confess that I had not realized that Guatemala was right next door. So I decided I would visit Guatemala. I took a taxi to the border where they informed me that I had to have a visa. I had to pay the taxi back to get the document, then pay again to get back to the border.

There I was in the middle of nowhere. I had to wait for a bus to come by to take me to Guatemala City. Guatemala is the third largest country of Central America. It shares a border with Chiapas, Mexico. On the Pacific side there exists a chain of volcanoes, some active. The country has suffered great eruptions and floods since its beginning. Seventy-five percent of the population are Indians, the Maya-Quiché.

The Indians were exploited during the Spanish conquest. Their condition has not improved greatly.

Guatemala City lies in a broad highland valley, that is very fertile from volcanic ash. It was founded in 1776, after Antigua was abandoned.

Antigua is in the south central part of the country. It is where the first two capitals were located. First was Cuidad Vieja situated at the head of a valley. Very near are two inactive volcanoes, Agua and Acatenango (12,982 feet) and Fuego which is active (12,854 feet). After its destruction, Antigua was founded at the same spot. At its height, it was a splendid city with churches, convents, monasteries, and luxurious homes, however, it suffered many disasters from floods, volcanoes, plagues, earthquakes and ecclesiastical scandals.

In 1773, two earthquakes leveled the city. A new capital was moved to what is now Guatemala City, an area supposedly safe from earthquakes. An earthquake destroyed this city in 1917 but it was rebuilt at the same spot.

Finally, the bus came. It was crowded so I had to stand part of the way. After arriving, I made some inquiries, ending up in a small hostel-like hotel.

This cosmopolitan city is very large. I just wanted to get on another bus as soon an possible for the famous market, Chichicastenango. Also, I wanted to visit Antigua, the original capital of Guatemala.

The next day, I boarded a bus for the market. This was an unusual experience. There were many crafts, exquisite materials in brilliant colors, and authentic designs and patterns woven by the Indians. Some items were embroidered. All of these things were jumbled among the wonderful produce grown in this fertile valley. A small stark white church presided over the market. This turned out to be a fascinating day. I even found a tiny restaurant where savory chicken was served. I dreaded getting back on the bus to return to Guatemala City.

Too soon, I was climbing off of the bus in the loud bustling city and walking to my hotel. I became disoriented by the clamor and confusion of this enormous city, bulging with humanity. I had to ask where my hotel was. As I walked along, I passed a scene which horrified me. I saw an ambulance parked across the street from me. A very young man was propped up against the wall of a building. He looked like he was only resting, or perhaps asleep. The men from the ambulance removed his body. I talked to the people standing near me. They said he was a refugee from Nicaragua, and had perished from starvation or other causes. They told me that this was a common occurrence. Many had entered from Nicaragua and met death. They were neither shocked nor disturbed. No one knew how long his body had been there before they finally came to remove it. I was almost ill. I hurried on to find my hotel. There were only about four other guests. I found peace and quiet and a nice meal. I did not want to venture out into the streets again.

This disturbing state of mind did not linger long. I was off for Antigua the next day. What a photographer's treasure! I spent the whole day wandering among some of the finest Spanish architecture. There were many extremely old weathered, crumbling buildings. They were majestic and magical to me because of the history and secrets encompassed in their aged walls. Likewise, the men who played a part in this era of conquest were intriguing.

One of these men was Bernal Díaz del Castillo (1492-1581). There was a metal plaque on the wall of one building, stating that this was where he wrote his famous chronicle, *The True History of the Conquest of New Spain,* published in 1632. This is a monumental work, written when he was at an old age. It is a fresh candid description of the men and the events he had witnessed while involved in the conquest. He served under several commanders before going to Mexico with Hernán Cortéz in 1519. This building where he produced his masterpiece was a masterpiece in itself for an artist. Here and there, weathering had destroyed plaster in places revealing various uneven patterns and textures of the stones underneath, There were the subtle hues of colors in the aged plaster. In front, passed an intermittent stream of modern present day Indians in their original traditional dress. I found a magnificent bronze bust, with an inscription honoring this man.

There were numerous churches, convents, cathedrals, and monasteries to film with the same weathered walls and facades. I saw many statues nestled in niches. I found one without a head. I climbed up on the roof of one building and could hear the priests singing a Gregorian chant. As their voices wafted upward toward me, the music produced strange deep emotions within me. I was lifted and carried back into hundreds of years long past. I really did not want to return.

This setting was breathtaking. These priceless colonial buildings had ornate facades with niches holding delicate statues. The many years had produced, on these walls and domes, huge cracks and lovely colors on the plaster which had entirely covered the large stones at one time. Now, in places, the innards of these ancient walls were exposed. This created incredible beauty for those artistically motivated. In the background, there were rolling green hills.

I went to a lovely hotel to have a bite to eat. A Latin band played out in the patio where I sat. Several gorgeous parrots were free to roam. One did acrobatics on an intricate web of metal cylinders, which served as perches. It was suspended from a tree and even had an umbrella. There was a net below which reminded me of the kind used in gymnastics to catch a fall. The other bird preferred to stand on a low ornately tiled wall, enclosing the tree. There were lush tropical plants and flowers growing at the base of the tree.

The time had come to jolt myself from this world of illusions—this fantasy. Another night in my small hotel, and then to locate a bus going back to Tapachula, Chiapas. The ride back was interesting. The countryside was lush green. We passed numerous volcanoes. We stopped for lunch at a market. There were stalls filled with every kind of pottery. Huge stacks of this were everywhere. Many stands were selling food to go. I grabbed something and climbed back on the bus. There was more green growth. Volcanoes soared toward the sky.

I found a modest hotel in Tapachula. I spent several nights here. A. bus carried me to the family of my friend. We spent several hours visiting. This is a very picturesque city. There was much to film, such as churches, statues, and colorful street scenes where the people were walking up and down the sloping streets. One evening, hundreds of small black birds perched on the wires just outside my hotel window. I have always wondered why. I became friends with two girls who worked in the hotel. It seemed as if we had known each other for a very long time. This was respite from Guatemala city.

I found myself in the small bus station, trying to get on a bus for San Cristobal de Las Casas. After a wait, there appeared a small dilapidated bus. I didn't know the vintage. A French couple, climbing on, helped me board with my heavy bag. They were speaking French. I tried desperately to remember something from my French classes at A.S.U. in 1943. *Merci beaucoup!* That was easy, but very little else came back to me.

The ride was absolutely beautiful, through pristine countryside. We passed among low hills and green mountains, and along a lovely river where a lone horseman was crossing. Fluffy white clouds were clinging to the sides of the mountains, with only their peaks peeking out. At one spot, a raging stream flowed by, filled with foam. What an idyllic interlude! We stopped at a shack by the side of the road and purchased tamales. They were the most delectable I have ever tasted.

It was pouring down rain when we arrived. A gentleman carried my bag as he directed me to a very nice hotel. It was very late in the evening.

The next day, I was off to photograph the small Indian settlement. The place was named after Bartolomé de Las Casas, whom I have mentioned earlier. He was Bishop of Chiapas from 1544 to 1547. This Spanish priest was extremely sensitive to the plight of the Indians during the Spanish Conquest.

There were the numerous churches and colorful markets. The inhabitants moving along the narrow streets provided ample material to film. I passed by four turkeys, with legs tied, stacked on a wall. They looked as if someone had dropped them there and gone off, forgetting them. I made my way out of town to see a new little church the Indians had built. It was distinctive, completely Indian in its architecture. There were simple lines, painted all white. They had used decorations of turquoise color. Around the doorway, bright turquoise tiles with many colored patterns formed a beautiful archway and entrance.

Three bells could be seen hanging in the rectangular tower. They were framed in three arched openings with the blue sky in the background. A simple cross was perched at the very top, in the center. It was flanked on each side by miniature turquoise domes with small white towers, each holding a tiny cross. Several Indians were puttering around the church, performing various tasks.

This was truly a trip of surprises. First, the finding of Guatemala on the doorstep of Tapachula, Chiapas. Next, I learned we would pass by Palenque on the way back to Vera Cruz. I had never heard of Palenque, the ancient city of Mayan architectural elegance, which seems to have grown out of its tropical environment.

I had to stop there. I found a very cheap hotel, and took a bus to the ruins. The first view of these ruins was breathtaking. The first structures I saw were a perfectly preserved pyramid-like building on the right side of the road and the partial view of a building with a dome at the end of the road. The green hills loomed up with misty shawls of white clouds on their shoulders. The structures appeared to be part of the tropical growth. They were so well adapted. I was reminded of the organic architecture of Frank Lloyd Wright. The buildings blended into the environment.

We saw sculpturing and paneling in low relief. This expression reached its height at Palenque. There are nearly life-sized figures carved in flowing lines and painted profusely. Surprisingly, throughout the many structures I saw the range of Mayan architecture which included ideas revived by later architects such as Francois Mansard, 1598-1666. The Maya had already used the Mansard effect, which is a curb roof having a lower slope almost vertical and an upper almost horizontal with the same profile on every side of the building.

On the bus trip back to Vera Cruz, I spent one night in Villa Hermosa in Tabasco. We arrived in pouring down rain. The next day, we passed huge bodies of water with little shacks nestled in the trees along the banks. Brightly colored clothes were hanging on lines suspended from one tree to another.

Back in Vera Cruz, I filmed the fishermen on the beach holding up their nets full of a variety of fish. There were many seascapes. Other men were just pulling in their nets. Many small boats dotted the harbor. Everyone who worked in the hotel had to have their picture taken.

One more night in the hotel—where I was well-known by then—and I was off for home. I planned to go to Vera Cruz again in December and take a bus to Catemaco. I had met someone at the bus station who told me about this place. He claimed it was a miniature Switzerland.

While waiting for December to come, I took a canoe trip with the Arizona Outdoor and Travel Club. We headed for the river. I was dressed all in white, carrying my camera and binoculars. We were supposed to see many eagles.

The group consisted of mostly novices at canoeing, including myself. Two professionals were conducting the trip. One very heavy-set man had just purchased a canoe. We reached the river and started loading up the canoes. I was told to ride with the gentleman in his new canoe. I stepped in gingerly and got settled. He was in the front. He stuck his oar into the bank to shove off, but instead of sitting erect, he leaned over too far. The canoe tipped over immediately. I found myself dumped into the water before we were even out into the river. I was soaking wet in my white outfit. I had tried to hold my camera and binoculars high. The camera got very wet, but the binoculars survived. This was very embarrassing to the owner of the new canoe and almost devastating to the man in charge of the outing. They were professionals, and were being paid as our guides. They dashed over to me and wrapped me in a blanket. I kept laughing it off and pretended to be having fun. In reality, I was miserable.

We were on our way down the river. It was beautiful. We did see some eagles. After several hours, we beached the canoes. Lunch was prepared for us. I was still wrapped in the blanket, but the lunch was delicious. The guides had gone out of their way preparing it. I had not regained my composure completely, but I did have a voracious appetite and was still trying to be a "good sport."

After lunch, we continued down the river. There was not much action on the shores, but we did spot several eagles and other birds. I still had not dried out. It was quite late when we came to the end.

We finally ended up at a campsite near the McDowell Mountains, north of Phoenix. I was still not in the best of shape. I set up my tent, pounded in the stakes, then joined the group for a shish kebab dinner cooked on a grill. They also prepared a peach cobbler cooked over the fire. It was marvelous.

As I crawled into my tent, I thought to myself, "Here you are so close to your warm cozy home. Why are you putting yourself through all of this?" We actually were not far from Phoenix. It was an experience I did not care to repeat. I tried to forget the shock of being dumped into the water before we even got into the river. I remember the tasty lunch and delightful dinner into which the guides put so much effort. I haven't been on a canoe trip since. I think I would prefer yachting, on a nice big boat.

Catemaco, Mexico—Christmas 1990

As I had planned, it was to be Christmas, 1990, in Catemaco, Mexico. My starting point was Vera Cruz, for the third time. It was great to see all of my friends at the same hotel where I had stopped before. I was like a relative returning. We had to go through the picture taking routine again. I have a wonderful family portrait of one employee with his wife and three precious children. After a year of my popping in and out, we had become very good friends.

I took a bus for Catemaco as soon as I could. It is near San Andrés Tuxtla, not very far from Vera Cruz. I found a hotel, but was not very happy with it. The next day I moved to another hotel very near the Laguna Catemaco. There was an excellent restaurant down the hill toward the lagoon, less than a block away. I took all of my meals here.

This was a small place. One could walk all through the city and along the lagoon. It was beautiful. There was much to photograph. I got some extraordinary pictures inside several churches that were lavishly decorated for Christmas.

One day, there was a small parade. Several people were dressed as animals. Others had on different costumes with grotesque masks. I never did understand what they were celebrating. It certainly wasn't a Christmas theme. The spectators on the sidewalks enjoyed the whole show with gusto. Many followed along behind the costumed people. It doesn't take much to completely delight the Mexicans.

This place certainly did not compare to Switzerland. Maybe my adviser, who had told me about it, had never been to Switzerland. However, it was charming. I found a huge cross with the crucified Christ hanging on it near the lake. One evening as I walked by, it was silhouetted against a setting sun. The dark cross stood up against the pale vermilion reflection from the sun in the lake behind it. Further, in the background, was a string of low black mountains. I found fishermen standing in their small boats, silhouetted in the same way, beneath canopies of huge trees growing at the edge of the lake. On the shore was a long line of nets, hanging on poles to dry. Numerous white sea birds were standing in clumps of green rushes. Aquatic herbs grew in the marshes along the shore.

One day, I went with some Mexican tourists in a boat to an unusual zoo. There was a monkey island inhabited by monkeys. We watched them moving all about among the shrubbery. Some came down to the edge. A few came down and just sat, looking us over. One was halfway in the water, taking a dip. Others were playing together. There was one tremendous crocodile in captivity. The guide taught all of us how to drink water from a banana leaf. Approaching the town, as we returned, we saw a picturesque skyline of churches and houses on the beach.

One day I hired a taxi to take me to their famous waterfall, Salto de Eyipantla. We had to walk down a trail to see the falls. They were beautiful and quite high, with large amounts of water crashing down. One part was a massive white foam-filled flow. There were several other smaller falls coming over the cliffs. It looked like a miniature Victoria Falls.

I wandered aimlessly through the markets, the streets, and along the waterfront. I passed women washing their vividly colorful clothes. Numerous laundry baskets of every color were parked haphazardly on the beach. After the washing, the clothes were spread out all over the shore to dry. While the women did their laundry, many nude children bathed and frolicked about. Wash day was enjoyed by all. I saw one beached boat filled with nude children sitting on the seats. I got photos of all these primitive scenes, which were quaint and full of richly graphic imagery. There was a charming aspect to the whole communal activity.

I happened upon a man leaning against a huge tree, soaking three wooden chairs in the waters. Two were lying on their sides and one on its back, They seemed almost animated, taking a dip. Two more chairs stood on the shore, propped against a tree. Another one, the man held in his hand preparing to immerse it. Why? I don't know. I guess everything can be washed in the lake.

As a matter of fact, there was constant activity along the shores of this lake. The fishermen were coming and going. A small lone boat was pulled up into the grass by the water with the oars still in it. No one was in sight. Many white birds were constantly standing along the water's edge, some fishing. Small ducks puttered in and out among the large white birds. During the day, there stood the large cross with Christ looking down upon this scene. Many looped fishing nets were hanging to dry. A wharf jutted out into the water. Along its sides the brightly colored boats lay, waiting to be manned.

One day I looked out of my hotel window upon a large garbage truck. It was full. Huge black birds were feasting on the refuse. One of them preferred to sit on the railing of my verandah. In his beak he held his share. It was an interesting profile.

One day I went to my regular restaurant below the hotel. The waiters kept telling me about a fish that they considered a delicacy. They praised it profusely. I tried it prepared three different ways. They had it listed on the menu in Spanish. I finally found out it was plain old carp. I had always believed that we threw this type of fish back into the water when caught, because of its bones and muddy flavor. I had to laugh about this, when a young man told me in English what kind of fish it was. Tactlessly, I told him we did not eat this fish. Three times I tried it, but could never find it to be the delicacy they insisted it was. They praised my persistence, but we could reach no agreement on the culinary attributes of this fish.

A huge pick-up truck was parked in the street. From a complicated iron webbing completely across the bed, there hung tremendous halves of beef and pork. The truck was full of this meat, just butchered. There was no refrigeration. I am sure it was on the way to the main mercado, also without refrigeration.

After filming more exquisite church interiors, I captured a young girl washing the windows at the hotel. She was dressed in a brightly colored blouse and skirt. She had a radiant smile on her face. I snapped her picture from the inside of the hotel, as she was lifting her brown arm high to wipe the window on the outside. Her uplifted face and smile were captivating. It was a joyful rendition.

It was time to go back to teaching. It was time to plan the next trip.

Windjammer Mania—1991

For Spring Break 1991, I decided to investigate the Windjammer Barefoot Cruises. This concept was dreamed up by a man known as Captain Mike. He had been in the Navy during World War II. It all started with six hundred dollars capital which he used to purchase the first vessel for what is now the world's largest fleet of "tall ships." Each ship he has added over the years has a fascinating story behind it.

I booked on the S/V *Flying Cloud,* sailing from Tortola and headed for ports of call in the British Virgin Islands in the Caribbean. This ship is a three-masted staysail schooner that was built in 1935 for the French Navy. It was used as a cadet training ship for twenty-five officers and one hundred cadets. Her maiden name was *Oisea des Isles* (Bird of the Islands), with her port in Papeete, Tahiti. During World War II, her name was changed to *Ave de Tahiti.* Her job was carrying nitrates. She also posed as a decoy during this war, spying for the Allied Forces. She received the Croix de Lorraine by General Charles de Gaulle for sinking two Japanese submarines.

After World War II, a Mexican company purchased her to carry cargo along the Baja coast. An official with the Mexican Consul had her converted to a sightseeing ship, providing sunset and dinner cruises around the Matzatlán, Mexico harbor. Losing his partner, the owner stripped her of everything valuable and left her aground in a Miami River.

In 1968, the *Flying Cloud* was acquired by the Windjammer fleet. She was completely rebuilt and refurbished in Miami. The holds for cargo became cabins, 110 volt electricity and air conditioning were installed. She had stained glass windows, rosewood benches, a spiral staircase, and a new charthouse. The original masts were wooden. A 1937 silver coin from New Zealand was found under the main mast, probably put there for good luck. She received all new masts and rigging. She has cruised from the Bahamas to Trinidad and Venezuela. Now her home port is in the Virgin Islands. She holds 67 passengers for a week in the sun, being cared for by a crew of 30. We sailed out of Tortola on this beautiful ship with sails. It was certainly a different delightful experience.

The history of the British Virgin Islands is a bit complicated. One thousand years before the arrival of Columbus, these islands were inhabited. Evidence points to the presence of Amerindians from the Ciboney tribe of Venezuela, around 300 B.C. Then they were conquered by the Arawaks about 200 A.D. It is believed that these islands were inhabited by Amerindian Arawaks for 400 years before the Europeans set foot on them.

The Arawaks had their origin on the banks of the Orinoco River in Venezuela. They were more advanced than the Ciboney tribe. They traveled about in well built canoes and were a peaceful people, engaging in fishing and farming. There have been archeological discoveries of their villages in Tortola and other islands. Their main enemy was the fearful Caribe Indians who had the reputation of massacring the men while they took over the women and villages.

Eventually, visions of a new trade route to India and the Middle and Far East stimulated and encouraged men like Christopher Columbus to find a new route. Columbus was determined. He and three ships set out to discover the "New World." After a successful return, the second voyage was planned for a year later. On this voyage, the ships were blown off course to Puerto Rico and actually anchored off Virgin Gorda. This name, translated "Fat Virgin", was given by Columbus. In fact, he named the entire archipelago "Las Once Mil Virgines." In this way, he didn't waste time trying to name each small island and inlet.

In the mid 1500's, rumors of the large amounts of gold to be found in the New World inspired and attracted pirates. There was a race and tug of war between France and Spain to gain this wealth. In reality, they were at war. Piracy flourished for many years in this region.

In 1542, the African slave trade started in the Caribbean. The Englishman, Sir John Hawkins, found slave trading to be profitable. In 1568, he was accompanied by Sir Francis Drake who later would return as Captain of a fleet of vessels whose purpose would be to raid the Spanish Galleons.

At this point, I must digress even further to write about Sir Francis Drake. I find him fascinating, and at the same time repugnant. He was the first Englishman to circumnavigate the globe. In 1572, he set out with two ships and seventy-four men for the first of his marauding expeditions. He captured the town of Nombre de Dios on the Isthmus of Panama, took over a ship in the harbor of Cartagena Colombia, burned Portobello, Panama, and seized three mule trains carrying thirty tons of silver. It is no wonder that he was favored by Queen Elizabeth. Secretly, she gave him permission to raid the places held by the Spanish on the West Coast. In the meantime Elizabeth maintained her friendship with Phillip II of Spain. This must have been the height of hypocrisy and deceit.

In 1577, Drake sailed with five ships, two of which he had to abandon in the Rio de La Plata, near Buenos Aires, Argentina. With the remaining three ships, he navigated the Straits of Magellan at the tip of South America. He was the first Englishman to accomplish this. The going wasn't easy. A terrible storm drove them southward. One ship and crew were lost. Another one separated from Drake and returned to England.

Drake continued on alone, in the *Golden Hind,* going up the coast of South America. He plundered Valparaiso, Chile and captured a treasure ship headed for Lima, Peru. Now, using the stolen Spanish charts, he went up the Pacific Coast as far as Washington state, returning to San Francisco to repair and provision his ship. He named the region New Albion, taking possession of it in the name of Queen Elizabeth. Albion was the ancient name of England.

He crossed the Pacific, visited the Philippines, Celebes, Java, and rounded the Cape of Good Hope at the tip of Africa. He arrived in Plymouth, England on September 20, 1580. The treasure he brought back has been estimated at 2,500,000 pounds. Abandoning her friendship with Spain, Elizabeth knighted Drake aboard his ship the *Golden Hind.*

In 1585, he took nineteen vessels and sacked Vigo, Spain, burned São Tiago in the Cape Verde Islands, and then crossed the Atlantic. Here he took Santo Domingo in Hispaniola, the island which was divided into Haiti and the Dominican Republic. He went on to capture Cartagena, Colombia and plundered the Florida Coast, including St. Augustine. He did, however, rescue Sir Walter Raleigh's Roanoke Colony, under Ralph Lane, on the Carolina Coast. This colony had not been doing well. Another colony came in 1597 under John White. White returned to England for supplies. When he came back to the colony in 1591 it had disappeared and is now known as the "lost colony." It is thought that the colonists, which included Virginia Dare the granddaughter of White, had perished from disease and Indian attacks. This mystery has not been solved.

In 1587, Drake entered the harbor of Cadiz, Spain with thirty ships and destroyed the Spanish fleet as they were assembling. He said he had merely singed the king of Spain's beard. He wished to continue this destruction of the Spanish ports, but Elizabeth would not condone it, however he was vice admiral in the fleet that defeated the Spanish Armada in 1588. Also, he was in joint command in an attempt to invade Portugal in 1589. They failed to take Lisbon.

His last expedition was with Hawkins in 1595 against the West Indies. The Spanish were prepared. It was a failure. Hawkins died off

Puerto Rico and soon afterward, Drake died of dysentery off Portobello, Panama. He was buried at sea.

The Spanish gradually lost their hold in the Caribbean. French, English, and Dutch ships moved in, bringing more slaves and taking back more treasures. In 1621, Tortola was known as Santa Ana when the Dutch settled in. They built a fort and challenged the Spaniards. In the mid 1600's, the Dutch introduced the cultivation of sugar cane. The methods used in Brazil were applied here with some success.

In the 1620's, the English had established colonies in the West Indies. Tortola was especially attractive to the British because of its position and the large amounts of timber on the island. The first Englishmen to come settled on Virgin Gorda, known then as "Paneston." The records show that the people were extremely poor and without law and order.

In the mid 1700's, there was economic growth. Cultivation on Tortola and Virgin Gorda produced 750,000 pounds of cotton and Jost Van Dyke was starting to harvest crops. Sugar cane was just getting started. Exports of cotton, sugar, and rum increased. During the French Revolution and Napoleonic Wars, many forts were built. This was the "golden age" for the plantations. Trade with the neighboring islands and America was booming. In 1774, about fifteen large sailing ships were busy with the trade between the Virgin Islands and England.

The Quakers began to arrive in the early 1720's, but there was a steady decline in their influence until 1762, when all religious meetings stopped. The Methodist missionaries arrived in the later part of the 1700's and established the first parochial school. The anti-slave movement gained momentum. Plantation owners began to be concerned about the number of slaves who were turning to religion and becoming aware of the educational opportunities.

In 1776, years before emancipation, a most unusual event occurred, Samuel and Mary Nottingham freed their twenty-five slaves, giving them an estate of fifty acres with the tools for cultivation. Abolition of the slave trade was approved by the English

Parliament in 1807, but freedom for the slaves did not come until August 1, 1834. This event is vigorously celebrated each year.

The sugar industry declined in the 1800's. Planters moved on and land prices depreciated. This allowed slaves to purchase their own small farms. In 1853, Cholera caused the death of 942 people. Smallpox took the lives of thirty-three more. Compulsory vaccinations were introduced. In 1867, a deadly hurricane and tidal wave destroyed all the houses and churches on Tortola. *The Royal Mail Steamship Rhone* sank and is a popular dive site today.

The British Virgin Islands prospered slowly and then in leaps and bounds. Now there is an adequate educational system and modern medical facilities. Tourism is booming, especially the yacht chartering and diving. The people voted in their own government in 1867.

In the morning, when they raised the sails of the *Flying Cloud*, "Amazing Grace" was played over the speaker. It brought tears to my eyes. We were off to our island-hopping.

Cooper Island, with Manchioneel Bay on the northwest coast, is a favored anchorage. The bay is named after a tree which grows a poisonous apple. We were warned not to eat the apple. Here we could surf or rent a kayak.

Jost Van Dyke, named for a female pirate, has lovely beaches. We were on our own. Norman Island inspired Robert Louis Stevenson to write *Treasure Island*. One is invited to snorkel and look for treasure hidden by pirateer Qwen Lloyd. This treasure was looted from the Spanish ship Nuestra Senora, and some was found in the caves of the island in the 1900's.

Peter Island was another port of call with beautiful beaches. Salt Island is where the *Rhone* sank and lies just off the coast. Tortola is the largest island and is the capital. Some of the best beaches are there, as well as trails leading up a hill for fantastic views.

My favorite island was Virgin Gorda. We hiked down to the baths to snorkel. There were huge boulders all along the water forming natural caves, grottos, and clear pools for snorkeling. After spending much time there, we hiked back up from the beach to a rustic restaurant. I had a shrimp sandwich that was delicious beyond description.

This trip turned out to be an unbelievable six days of sunning, sailing, snorkeling, and sumptuous eating.

I was so enchanted, I started making plans for another Windjammer getaway. Meanwhile, I won a six day trip with a coupon which came in the mail. I dashed to my travel agent. She made several phone calls and got me reservations for two six day trips back to back.

In August 1991, I was off for Grenada for the two cruises in the Grenadines. Grenada is in the Windward Islands which are the southern group of the Lesser Antilles in the West Indies. This is an archipelago of tiny islands strung out between St. Vincent and Grenada. They are of volcanic origin and are rugged, mountainous, and well forested with streams and lakes. From the time Columbus discovered Grenada in 1498 until the French came to settle in 1650, the island was not colonized. It was left to the aboriginal inhabitants, the Caribes. It changed hands between the English and the French, but in 1783 it became British.

We were to sail on the S/V *Yankee Clipper* which was built in 1927 and named *Cressida*. Alfred Krupp, a German industrialist, had it built to be his private yacht. It was one of the few armor-plated private yachts in the world. She was confiscated during World War II and later acquired by the Vanderbilts. She was renamed *Pioneer,* and considered one of the fastest tall ships. In 1965, she joined the Windjammer Fleet, being christened *Yankee Clipper.*

When we arrived in Grenada, we were welcomed and entertained by a group of natives in colorful costumes. St. George's Harbor is most picturesque. In the outdoor marketplace we noticed the aroma of fresh spices. Cinnamon, nutmeg, and mace are grown locally. They are used abundantly in the local restaurants. This island is called "Spice Island." There are lush green mountains, waterfalls, and lakes. I hired a young man to take me to Concord Falls. It was beautiful. He also plucked some nutmeg from a tree for me to take home.

Again, we island-hopped. Carriacou with its deserted beaches and the small crescent- shaped island of Canouan, with only a small population of farmers and fishermen, were two where we anchored. I was amazed at the peaceful unspoiled beauty. Mayreau has one road, one pickup truck, and more animals than people. Palm Island, which has over one thousand palm tress, was a treasure. Magnificent beaches framed all of these islands. We went ashore on one tiny island that had not one inhabitant. We spent the whole day sunning and swimming. A tremendous outdoor meal was prepared on the beach for us.

At one stop we ambled all around an old fort. There I perched on an antiquated cannon. One of the most interesting islands was Bequia. This is one of the last legal whaling ports. There is ship building right on the beaches. One builder was standing by his unfinished boat. It was almost a skeleton, but was coming along. He was proud of his craft . . . and *craft*. He was anxious to be filmed leaning against the hull. There were many picturesque views on the island.

I filmed a virtual dollhouse there. It was a little square, red house with white trim, on the water. There was a double set of stairs, one on each side leading up to the front, white trimmed door at the entrance. White lace-like trim was on the triangular cupola above the door. It was adorable.

One day, three enormous black fishermen in a lovely sleek blue fishing boat pulled up alongside our ship. One was a hulk of a man. He was dressed only in red bikini trunks, with his hair done in the style of the Rastafarians of Jamaica. Their catch of five big beautiful fish lay on the floor of the boat. Our cook climbed down into their boat. He examined the fish and made his choice. He held the fish up and handed it to another crewman. This fish was prepared for us. We really had a fresh catch.

We had music on board. A group of different people were organized from the crew and passengers. There were several guitar players. The drummer was a huge handsome black man with a full black beard. Someone played the violin. The Captain played the banjo. They were seated on the deck, playing as we sailed along.

We stopped at St. Vincent. It was more populated and did not have the charm of the other islands. We did find a post office where we could buy stamps. Also, we were boated out to a huge rock from which we snorkeled.

These twelve days of being a beach bum and a beachcomber were truly a magnificent and memorable experience. My first urge was to live like this forever as a child of the sea. I wanted to stay on the beaches where the windswept palms leaned over the sand and crashing waves. Then reality clicked in. No, I guess I wasn't programmed for this type of existence. I faltered as I was returning home. With much nostalgia, I look back to those wonderful days and nights on the tall ships.

Kino Bay—Thanksgiving 1991

Every year, members of the Arizona Outdoor and Travel Club climb on a bus and head for Mexico. They go to the area near Los Cabos and the Sea of Cortez, the Gulf of California. The first time I went with them, they were going to Kino Bay. They loaded the bus with clothing for the Seri Indians, who live near this bay.

The Seris live in several villages thirteen to forty miles north of Kino Bay. The largest settlement is El Desemboque. They are famous for their ironwood carvings of birds and fish and their basket weaving.

According to some, the Seris were cannibalistic. One author describes his visit to the island of Tiburon. He saw some Seri Indians who were living in caves near the water's edge. A skiff was lowered for a friendly visit, but as they neared shore, about a dozen savage-looking men and women dashed out of the caves carrying shark spears. The group headed back for the big boat quickly. The Mexican crew, who had refused to accompany the shore party, explained that some natives shipwrecked on Tiburon had disappeared. This was in 1956. Cannibalism was suspected. Up to this time, two groups of Seri had been allowed by the Mexican Government to stay on the island with the condition that they give up cannibalism. in 1956, with the mysterious disappearance of two Mexican fishermen, the Mexican Army moved the whole Tiburon population of two hundred and twenty to the mainland.

Since their coming to the mainland, the Seri men hunted turtles for the market and sometimes worked on farms. Now, they are in the fishing business. They keep their tribal habits and live in small huts made of sticks. Thin flea-bitten dogs prowl all around. The girls and single women continue to paint their faces with brightly colored stripes. They start just below the eyes and cover the nose and lower part of the face, resembling the veil of Moslem women. Our guide warned the men in our party to run if they saw a woman approaching with her face made up like this. It means she is available. He also assured us that now the Indians are perfectly safe to visit, if they don't appear to be hungry. So we visited.

Our leader and a few from our group, including me, climbed into a van with all of the clothing. We drove the few miles to their village. The leader knew the matron well, as he had made such a delivery before. They were thrilled to see us.

The attractive matriarch was definitely in charge. Everyone gathered around us. Our leader and the matron started out keeping the distribution of clothing and other items orderly. Toward the end, there seemed to be a burst of enthusiasm and an uncontrollable determination to be on the receiving end. Bob, the leader, was inundated at one point. I could barely see him. Proverbial mayhem reigned. I felt a little uncomfortable, as an altercation broke out among the recipients. The issue seemed to be that several women had received more than their share. We had a few tense moments. Eventually our van was emptied. After a short visit we left, but not before I filmed some fishermen holding up a very big fish. Actually, a beautiful little boy was holding up the big one. They were very pleased and proud. The Seri were a childlike, friendly people. I don't think I believe that story about cannibalism. When I got home, I mailed a large oilskin slicker and hat for bad-weather fishing to one of the fishermen. Of course, I included copies of the photos I had taken of them. This had to be one of the most unusual experiences of my life.

Back at Kino Bay, we spent time on the beach and ambled through the town. The place where the fishermen congregated was the most exciting. I circulated among them, filming them holding up their catch. There was a multitude of sea gulls and pelicans clamoring on the beach. The sky and beach were thick with them. I almost felt as if I was being attacked. They were attracted to all the fishing boats, which probably supplied them with a free lunch now and then.

A lovely typical Thanksgiving dinner was prepared for us at a very nice local restaurant. It included turkey. It was memorable.

Four days went fast. We climbed on our bus to go home. We did stop at several Mexican towns on the way back to sightsee and have lunch. Arriving back home very late in the night, it was hard to not believe that all was but a dream.

Amazon—Spring Break 1992

We arrived March 21, 1992 in Iquitos, Peru by Faucett Airlines. This city is the gateway to the discovery of the Amazon and resembles a typical frontier outpost. From the air flying in, there are endless expanses of green unexplored tropical forests. In the city itself, I saw the richly colored tiles on the facades of many buildings, reminiscent of the rubber boom years. This city was founded in 1863. It is 2,300 miles from the mouth of the Amazon. It is the farthest inland port of considerable size in the world. Some ocean vessels, which draw no more than fourteen feet, can reach it.

The jungle is a wilderness filled with many species of plants and animals which have not been scientifically classified. Some coffee, cottons timbers, and tagua nut are exported. The wild rubber boom began in the 20th Century, then the market collapsed. The Andes are a great barrier to the transporting of goods to the Pacific. Now the trade is mostly carried on by way of the Atlantic.

The tagua nut is the fruit of the ivory-nut palm. These trees get about twenty feet high and can live to be one hundred years old. It produces a pod containing up to forty or more nuts, one to two inches in diameter. The nuts are of a white or cream color and are very hard. They are sold as a substitute for ivory. Many have been shipped to the United States and Europe for the manufacture of buttons and other small items. They can be tested to see if they are ivory by applying sulfuric acid to them. The acid turns the tagua to a reddish color, but does not affect ivory.

The Iquitos Indians live here. The tribes are perfectly adapted to their environment, carrying on very well long before civilization appeared. They have a fascinating folklore and very effective medicinal practices.

We were transported to our hotel very late at night and dinner was not provided. I don't even remember eating.

The next morning, we boarded a thatched-roof launch (pamacaris), for an hour's ride to the Amazon Camp on the Momon tributary. We took a delightful first walk in the jungle and were served lunch. On the walk, we passed a variety of tropical trees and flowering plants. We came upon three trees growing from the same spot. Two pale green trunks and a mottled gray trunk were pressed against each other like Siamese triplets joined together. At their bases there was a giant black furry spider tied up for the tourists. All around were tropical plants with huge, darker green leaves. They were as shiny as if they had been waxed. Among this green profusion, lovely bright red flowers with yellow centers emerged. Another plant with smaller pale green leaves displayed a magnificent fuchsia colored flower.

A brightly colored parrot sat on our launch as we boarded to head back to get on our boat, the M/V *Area*, for the 5:00 P.M. sailing. All the passengers had to walk down a flight of stairs toward the boat. The steps were primitive and broken down. We all hung on to the wobbly railing which was intermittently intact. I was astounded that the owners of the boat could take such a risk, having their passengers pass down to the boat in this way. It would have been so easy to fall.

The boat was no luxury liner. It was small and very old. However, my brochure said it was refurbished and designed for cruising the Amazon. It had eighteen twin cabins and one single cabin, five shared bathrooms, enclosed dining room, covered lounge/bar, and a large sun deck. We were off, gliding down the wide muddy river.

The first night, I was confined to my bunk bed with a fever. I think it may have been a reaction to the required Yellow Fever shot. I was not well at all.

The next morning, I was still alive and ready for the early morning bird watching and a visit to a Yagua Indian village. We pulled into shore to observe the Indians with their blow pipes. The women had grass-like skirts on and were nude from the waist up. Both men and women demonstrated the use and accuracy of the blow pipes. These are long poles which they hold up to their mouths to blow the darts. When hunting for food, these would be poisoned darts. Evidently, they are very efficient, since they have been in use for many years.

Off again we floated, passing lush tropical growth. Along the way, we would see an occasional small thatched hut, perched on stilts to avoid the flooding of the river. One of these was extremely picturesque. It was on the bank, silhouetted perfectly in the water. A canoe with two men was nestled in the trees at one side. It was a charming photo. As we continued on, we passed a settlement. There were sixteen children of all ages standing on the bank watching us go by. Three natives' canoes were beached with children sitting in them.

We stopped at Pevas, the oldest Peruvian town on the Amazon. We walked around. I was amused to see a typical forest house with an old Singer sewing machine perched on the balcony. I had to have a picture of this sight. It was so incongruous with the surroundings.

In a large communal dwelling, we witnessed men and women dressed in clothing made from white bark on which were painted vivid decorations. They performed for us.

Then there was an afternoon hike through the dense rain forest in the Shishita River area. Topping off the day, we climbed into one of the small launches from the ship. We traveled through flooded creeks and lagoons in the dense forest to hear the night sounds of the jungle.

The following day, there was an expedition to observe the Victoria Regis water lilies. We cruised in and out of the forest. Back into the main river, we saw the most amazing thing I could possibly dream of—pink dolphins. I didn't know they existed. They were emerging, then submerging constantly, right in front of the ship.

We saw a native canoe being built. The men were carving out the inside of a log from a large tree. There were piles of wood chips lying all over the ground around the place of construction. It was almost finished. It was fascinating. What an ingenious way to make a boat.

As our boat moved along, we kept passing families on the bank. They were clustered together under huge trees. The women and older children were all holding babies. One of these trees had bloomed. The blossoms had fallen on the ground on a large area all around the base of the tree. It formed a brilliant pink carpet. There was a dark pink diminishing into lighter shades of pink where the rays of sunlight reached.

We stopped at the missionary village at Lake Caballococha and mingled with the people. A few were wearing the grass skirt attire for the tourists, including three small boys.

As we moved along, small canoes pulled up frequently to the side of our ship. They were filled with baskets of fish and multicolored produce such as bunches of green bananas stacked among the red fruits and assortment of vegetables.

There was even a piranha fishing excursion. There we were sitting in the launch, holding our primitive fishing poles over the water. I had my usual bad luck fishing, not even a bite, but it was fun. The guide caught a piranha. I have a picture of him holding a large one, propping the mouth of the fish open with his fingers to display the dangerous and often fatal teeth. The bartender on the boat had a flourishing business selling piranha heads. He cut the heads off of the body, cleaned them, and dried them. Then he applied a type of varnish. I couldn't resist. I bought two of them for seven dollars. They are on display to this day, on a bookcase in my family room, keeping the huge beetle from Honduras company.

After sunset, we crossed a lake in the launch to look for caimans in the reedy shallows of the lake. There must have been a shortage of these creatures. I do not have one photo of a caiman.

We proceed to move down the wide river. Early in the morning, we arrived at the frontier with Colombia and Brazil, the twin cities of Leticia and Tabatinga. Leticia is a very small town, right on the river. The shoreline was lined with booths of the mercados. Everything was being sold. There were fruits, vegetables, clothing, and a large open case propped open, displaying cigarettes and candy. Stacks of platanos were everywhere. Freshly caught fish were sprawled out over a monstrous wooden platform. Several fishermen held up large dangling fish to attract a buyer. Another wooden platform was covered with eight tremendous fish that had been dressed. There was a huge jumble of produce and fish, and people milling all around.

We took a short walk to view a pool filled with the gigantic floating leaves of water lilies. Some of the leaves appeared to be more than two feet in diameter. They covered the surface of the water like huge saucers, forming an unusual pattern. Then we found a nice restaurant. Nearby, a young girl held a brilliantly colored toucan on her arm. We sat at the outdoor table and had refreshments. I had to take a bus into Brazil, where I had lived for two years. I was looking for the Brazilian "farinha," a flour made from manioc.

The next day, we had a launch trip on the Antiquari River to try our luck at fishing again in a small backwater lake. As usual, I had nothing to show for this exertion. In the afternoon, we stopped at a remote leper hospital in San Pablo. There was a gift shop selling handicrafts of the patients. We didn't give up on our search for caimans. We went on a night cruise on the Mayaruna River to listen to the nocturnal sounds emitting from the jungle and to seek the evasive caiman.

The morning arrival at Pijuayal is where we cleared customs. We continued up to the Ampiyacu River to spend time in the Bora and Huitoto Indian villages. We mingled with the natives and witnessed dance demonstrations. Being a schoolteacher, the visit to their primitive schoolhouse fascinated me. The desks were large wooden planks held up on hefty sections of logs serving as legs. The benches were of the same design. I was emotionally moved by this little schoolhouse. I had to have someone take my picture seated at a desk. Photos of the teachers and school children were a must. Most of the children were dressed in grass skirts and shirts. It was a poignant scene which I shall cherish.

We were right on schedule headed back to Iquitos. Then our ship crashed into a tremendous tree lying along the bank of the river. Something in the engine had been damaged. They tried to get it started, to no avail. So a perky little red hydroplane was ordered to take the passengers to Iquitos to catch their planes. No luggage could be taken as the plane was so small. This was a memorable event. We all stood clustered together on the bank, waiting for the plane to arrive. It was hot. At last, a precious bright red plane glided across the river toward us. We were loaded on and took off for Iquitos. The town looked like home, even without our belongings. It was good to see the unique taxis running up and down the streets again. They consisted of a small motorcycle with four wheels, carrying a good-sized passenger compartment behind. It looked like a modern rickshaw. The man driving replaced the Chinese coolie. There were many going up and down the streets, day and night.

Our luggage had to wait until Faucett flew into Iquitos again. They did not want to send it through Lima, fearing it would be lost or stolen. I arrived home safe and sound. My suitcase arrived several weeks later, in good shape. When I started unpacking however, I found four lovely large Indian carvings from balsa wood. There was a fish, a whale, an armadillo, and a turtle. I was stunned when I realized the little turtle was wearing a real tortoise shell. Being a biologist and an environmentalist, I was abashed and aghast.

Canyonlands—April 1992

Since I was not going to Africa until June 13th, I decided to take my first four-wheel trip to Canyonlands with The Arizona Outdoor and Travel Club. I knew for sure that I didn't want to get involved in another canoe excursion, after my last experience.

Rather late one day, we started driving toward the Utah border. We passed through some very rugged country near the end as we drove toward our destination. Unfortunately, it was very dark and we missed getting a good look at the scenery. Finally, we stopped to camp on a plateau with scrub junipers. It was late and pitch black. I staggered around, trying to set up my tent. I was looking for rocks with which to pound in the stakes.

The next morning was an eye-opener. We looked out on a great variety of red and white natural sandstone monuments of all shapes and sizes, carved by water and wind erosion. There were huge pinnacles and mushroom-shaped structures. There were arches and natural bridges. In some areas, tremendous flat boulders covered the ground over a large expanse. It was like a wonderland—another world.

Canyonlands National Park on the Colorado Plateau is a true wonder, filled with a unique diversity of beauty, almost beyond description. You have to see it to believe it. This landscape was created by the deeply cut canyons of the Green and Colorado Rivers. Every arroyo and wash flow into the Colorado River which has carved down through three hundred million years accumulation of rock layers. One finds the Needles, which are serrated rows of sandstone spires rising from grass covered land. There are a series of steep-walled canyons called The Grabens. They appear in rows resembling streets. Fascinating names have been given to each in this assortment of sculptures formed by erosion such as: the Doll House tottering on the edge of Cataract Canyon; the Land of Standing Rocks; the Maze; Upheaval Dome; Hatch Point Mesa; and Island in the Sky. The canyons have their own names such as Elephant, Lost, Squaw, Big Spring, Horse, and Cataract Canyon. Each one conceals its own singular set of arches, springs, rock art, and ruins in numerous tortuous side canyons.

This is a geologist's paradise. We are dealing with different layers of sediments which tell the story of the last 300 million years. The Law of Superposition enters here. This is the principle that, except in extremely deformed strata, horizontal layers of sedimentary rocks overlying another bed are always the younger. This seems extremely obvious, but it took a Danish court physician living in Italy in 1669 to propose this idea. He was Nicolaus Steno. There is layer upon layer of sedimentary rocks in deep reds, browns, and soft off-whites.

The oldest rocks are called the Paradox Formation. These underlie the whole region, but are hidden in many parts of the park by younger formations. Thousands of feet of salt, precipitated by a deep shrinking ocean basin once situated in southeastern Utah, now make up the bulk of these beds.

In the upper Cataract Canyon, the presence of marine limestone and shale is named the Elephant Canyon Formation. There is evidence that the sea returned to Canyonlands. There once existed a great highland to the northeast. Streams flowed from there through Canyonlands to a western sea. There was an oscillating shoreline where sandbars became sandstone, as did windblown coastal dunes.

The sediments carried down from the highlands collected as shale and mudstones.

The most vivid colors are found in the red and white bands of the Needles. These beds are in the Cutler Formation, younger than the Elephant Canyon Formation. At a later date in time, we found what is called the Moenkopi Formation, which indicates that a widespread shallow sea was present. Ripple marks, mud cracks, and in some instances fossil footprints of reptiles and amphibians were found there.

After this sea retreated, the rest of the sediments of Canyonlands were continental in origin. This means they were deposited on land. All layers above Moenkopi are non marine.

We found the Chinle Formation tucked in between the Moenkopi and the large orange cliffs which hold up the mesa. Here, the steep slopes of the Chinle rise up. This formation is made up of cliff-forming Moss Back sandstone, bearer of uranium. Above this, appear gray and red mudstones. The most well known bed of the Chinle is the Petrified Forest Member named for the petrified wood occurring in the clays.

Above the Chinle, are the massive sandstones named Wingate, Kayenta, and Navajo. Wingate is the oldest and Navajo the youngest. These crown Canyonlands, forming high cliffs that rim the river basins. The dune deposits of the Wingate form the vertical walls of the mesas, looking like a brownish orange barrier. The more resistant Kayenta caps these walls protecting them from erosion. This formation is a light colored sandstone deposited by rivers. Next on top is the Navajo which is made up of ancient sand dunes. All the younger rocks deposited over Canyonlands have disappeared due to erosion and uplift which formed this place.

Many changes have occurred in this land over millions of years. One example is the thick salt beds in the oldest formation. Paradox, under the pressure of thousands of feet of rock, accumulated on top. The salt oozed and slowed upward, changing the layers above it. Salt, being less dense than the rock, rose up and domed the rocks on top.

These are called salt domes or salt anticlines, and are characteristic of Canyonlands.

In some instances, erosion penetrated the sedimentary rocks overlying the salt intrusion so that the groundwater could reach the salt, dissolving it. Then the domed layers, losing their support, collapsed forming large salt valleys. We saw these to the north and east of Canyonlands. Upheaval Dome is a dramatic example of how this process can transform the land.

There are other anticlines such as this from which potash salts are extracted from the salty core of the anticline. This process is known as the solution process. River water is pumped down through the dome and then up into large evaporation ponds.

The Colorado River actually meanders along the course of a salt anticline, which appears to control the course of the river. From the residue of the dissolved Paradox salts, large deposits of gypsum are found along the river.

This deeply buried Paradox salt has also played a role in the faults and joints (parallel cracks) which formed the Needles and the Grabens. When the salt flowed out, brittle layers of rock were shattered into cracks called faults and joints. Along larger faults, huge blocks dropped down creating instant valleys called grabens.

There are two reasons why I found it necessary to digress into the geology of Canyonlands. In the first place, the names of the formations intrigue me. Secondly, the traces and their origin found in each formation is fascinating. The area is like a huge layered cake. The intermittent icing is made up of the caps which are the more resistant rocks.

The Green and the Colorado Rivers created Canyonlands. Each river continues to grind down through the layers. Rushing waters undercut walls which fall from the force of gravity. There are floods in the sidestreams which contribute to this process of erosion by washing away rockfalls into the river.

No dams have been constructed on the Green and Colorado for miles upstream from Canyonlands. So we see the powerful wild river coming down places like Cataract Canyon. It is untamed with muddy raging torrents at certain times of the year. All of the arroyos collect water from the many cracks. This produces foamy red streams carrying away Canyonlands.

We climbed into our four-wheel vehicles and started putting them to the test. For two days we drove on barely passable routes. We went up and down among these enormous sculptures produced by nature. I could not believe where the drivers took their vehicles. Nothing was impossible. At moments I was completely terrified. In fact, most of the time I was in this state. My driver was a dear eighty year old man who had had a large portion of his colon removed. Nothing stopped him. Sometimes passengers from one vehicle had to get out and direct the other vehicles to avoid rupturing a gas tank or an oil pan. Up and down we went, creeping over the massive rocks and through the passes of the Grabens.

Among all of these geologic marvels of every shape conceivable, we would pass, now and then, a clump of exquisite cacti. It would be nestled in the rocks displaying bright red flowers. All the other growth in our area consisted of scrub trees and bushes. From time to time, there rose up the black gnarled skeleton of a tree, still reaching up majestically toward the heavens, even in death. The variety of the formations and the extent and size of the massive flat shelves of rock was incredible.

My driver and I found remnants of an Indian house, made of flat rocks upon flat rocks. It nestled in a crevice cave between monstrous boulders. At one stop, we saw a large rock wall covered with petroglyphs. It was a jumble of animals such as goats, deer, and the horses. There was a maze of abstract symbolic Indian designs in the background.

On our way out, on the last day, we came down the Staircase in our vehicles. It was literally an enormous stairway made up of huge slabs of rock. It was steep. I closed my eyes most of the time. Then we dropped down on a completely vertical road into a large parking area.

We were on our way home. My first four-wheel trip had put me through some frightening moments. It was a fantastic experience.

Upon arriving home, I ran to my Arizona Outdoor and Travel schedule, and frantically searched to see when there was another four-wheel excursion planned.

Epilogue

I was off again the next month, May, 1992. It was to the red rocks of Sedona, Arizona. It too was rugged and beautiful, but only a one day trip. It was obvious I had experienced the most unusual and terrifying events on my first trip. By then I was a four-wheel addict.

Africa—June 12, 1992
Kenya-Tanzania

At last, I am headed on an African tour with Safariworld. I left from New York on the KLM Royal Dutch Airlines. Our destination was Amsterdam. I was certainly looking forward to the next two weeks. We had a three hour layover there. I ate a sandwich that was not very tasty, and hung around the airport. I didn't go into town because I had been there several times before. We didn't leave for Nairobi, Kenya until two o'clock in the afternoon. We arrived in Nairobi at one thirty A.M. We were escorted to the Safari Park Hotel. It was a fabulous hotel. A monstrous life-sized elephant with long tusks stood in the middle of the lobby. There was a huge fireplace and lovely furnishings. We had plenty of time to examine all of this as there seemed to be some confusion. We were actually waiting for my roommate to appear. She never came, so they moved a twin bed into a room to accommodate me. All of us stood around in the lobby for quite awhile. I didn't get to bed until four in the morning. They found out that my dear roommate had cancer and was not able to make it. This saddened me in one respect, but, in another way I was happy to be receiving single accommodations for the rest of the trip. I thought to myself that this was one of those cases where a person has a dream, but waited too long to fulfill it. It haunted me.

I must take time now to give a brief history of the geography of Kenya. It is a country on the east coast of Africa which straddles the equator. On the north it has a border with Sudan, Ethiopia, and Somalia. To the west is Uganda and to the south Tanzania. The Indian Ocean is on its east coast. Mt. Kenya is the highest peak at 17,058 feet. It has snow throughout the year and frequent cloud cover. Mount Kilimanjaro with an elevation of 19,340 feet is just over the border of Tanzania to the south.

Geographically, the country has four main regions: The Northern and Eastern Plains; the Western Plateau; the Rift Valley and Central Highlands; and the Coastal Belt. Kenya has a diversity of scenery and is thought to be one of the most beautiful countries of Africa. One sees the snow-capped peaks of Mt. Kenya, tropical forests, lush grasslands, and the coral beaches on the coast. Inland are the great plains of Africa where great numbers of elephants, giraffes, zebras, lions, cheetahs, rhinos, wildebeests, leopards, and hippos were seen. There are many other types of wildlife besides the ones listed above.

Kenya's history goes back at least 2,500,000 years. There have been fossil discoveries at lake Turkana to the north and at Olduvai Gorge in Tanzania. The Leakey family made some discoveries that are said to be the earliest human relics found in the world.

Merchants from the Roman Empire sailed along the coast of Kenya in the second century. Trading was carried on in villages established by Arab traders, who had arrived earlier. Traders came from India, Persia, China and Arabia. The main exports were ivory, spices, tortoise shells, and slaves. The coastal villages were in places like Mombasa and Lamu which could be defended easily. Towns flourished and major cities were established by the 12th century.

Vasco de Gama, the Portuguese explorer, arrived in Mombasa in 1498. After numerous raids, the Portuguese were forced out by the Arabs and went south to Mozambique.

Inland, the Bantu speaking people entered Kenya from the south and from Sudan came the Nilotic people. Other tribes coming in were the Masai, the Samburu, the Turkanas, and the Kalenjin. Hamitic tribes from Somalia and Ethiopia arrived. Many became farmers as did the Europeans who came in the 1900's.

There were the Mau Mau terrorist activities in 1952. Kenya came under African rule in 1961. Independence was granted in 1963. Kenya became a republic of the British Commonwealth. Jomo Kenyatta was the first president. He died in 1978. Daniel Arap Moi took over.

There are over forty different African tribes which can be divided into four main ethnic groups: Bantu, Nilotic, Nilo Hamitic (Masai and Turkana), and Hamitic (Somali). Each tribe is very different in appearance, character, and culture.

Swahili is one of the several hundred Bantu languages spoken throughout the southern half of Africa. The word, Swahili, comes from an Arabic word meaning "coast." Ki-Swahili is the national language of Kenya.

The dominant religion is Christianity. In the rural areas traditional religions are practiced. Along the coast, Islam is the dominant element and numerous Mosques are to be found.

After a short night's rest, we were served a magnificent breakfast in the unusual restaurant situated out on the grounds of the hotel. We were then asked to attend a safari briefing which seemed to drag on a bit. We were anxious to get started. They provided each of us with a handsome large tote bag. We had to leave our luggage stored at the hotel when we took off in the vehicles. I misunderstood and ended up putting the beautiful tote-bag in my luggage and the essentials in plastic laundry bags from the hotel. This was very embarrassing for me when we finally got on the road. Everyone was packed in their handsome totes. I was carrying two laundry bags. To this day, I don't know how I could have been so confused about this arrangement.

After the lengthy meeting, we left for a sightseeing tour of the city of Nairobi, including the National Museum. Then we proceeded to the home of Karen Blixen in the Ngong Hills. Lunch was in the garden.

Karen Blixen was a Danish authoress who usually wrote in English and under a pseudonym. She married Baron Blixen in 1914 and went to live in Kenya on a coffee plantation until 1931. She wrote two books in the genre of the German romances of the 18th century, *Seven Gothic Tales* (1934) and *Winter's Tales* (1943). She also wrote a political allegory, first published in German-occupied Denmark, *The Angelic Avengers* (1947). The book was written under the pseudonym of Pierre Andrezel. The most well known of her books is the autobiographical *Out of Africa* (1937), written under the name of Isak Dinesen. This was during the time when there were not many women writers and those who tried to write were not held in particularly high esteem.

The Blixen home was charming. We were guided carefully throughout with information about every room and every item in it. Her life was touched upon, also. She is highly regarded here and there was almost a feeling of reverence demonstrated by the woman guide. This was carried to the point of rudeness when several tourists happened to touch the untouchable or step out of the roped areas. The grounds around the house were spacious and enchanting with beautiful blooming trees. We ate our lunch gathered around three large round tables pushed together, outside in the garden.

From here, we went to the Utamaduni Artisan center in Langata, and to the Giraffe Manor. We saw two very large giraffes with their baby and were invited to feed them.

In the evening, we were escorted to the home of a prominent colonel and his wife. It was raining when we arrived. Their hospitality was overwhelming. We were served a delicious dinner in the patio/garden, in spite of the rain. It was a lovely personal experience.. They hosted all twelve of us as if we were family.

We were very excited the next morning as we boarded our safari van. We headed south toward the Masai Amboseli Game Reserve. I climbed on with my two plastic laundry bags holding my belongings. We passed through rather flat countryside on our way to the marshland where elephants sometimes travel in herds of over two hundred. Mt. Kilimanjaro rises 19,340 feet in this area, but unfortunately the cloud cover prevented us from ever getting a view of this famous mountain.

We had lunch at the Amboseli Serena Lodge where we were to spend the night. The food was lavish. At last we were to go for our first game viewing in the park. We climbed into our vehicle which had an open section in the roof so that you could stand and prop yourself up to photograph the animals. I could not believe this was happening to me. I had never experienced such excitement as this.

We passed many small comical looking monkeys sitting around. They were grayish monkeys with a yellowish tinge on the dorsal part of their bodies. Their chests and abdomens were white. They had black faces with white cheek tufts and a white bar above their eyes that looks like a headband. Their lower legs were of a dark color which gave the impression they were wearing black stockings. These monkeys are widespread throughout East Africa. They are diurnal and arboreal as well as terrestrial. They are gregarious and often travel in large troops.

The brochures had not exaggerated! We traveled over the large grass-covered expanse of marshland for several hours. We saw herds of zebra and wildebeest. The wildebeest is also known as the White-Bearded Gnu. It is a heavy, ungainly looking antelope with a humped back, buffalo-like horns, and a long black mane and tail. It also has a distinct beard on the throat. There were also numerous groups of elephants always surrounded by small white egrets. These birds ride around on the elephant eating the insects harbored in its hide.

Dinner was another sumptuous affair, but was interrupted abruptly by the appearance of a baby hippopotamus walking up on the lawn towards the large glass windows of the restaurant. It was very dark outside, but some lights lit up the yard. All of the tourists went berserk jumping up from their tables and dashing to the window. I didn't have my camera which furiously frustrated me.

After dinner, I returned to my precious little room with window plants and red twin beds. The furnishings and pictures on the wall were unique. I could hardly wait for the 5:00 A.M. call in the morning for a pre-breakfast game drive.

After breakfast, we headed for the Tanzanian border where we were to change safari guides. At the border there was a great crowd of people, many of whom approached us. Some were selling items and others were merely curious about us. They seemed to be swarming over us. There was much confusion as we went through customs. We said goodbye to our guide and greeted the new guides.

We drove to Arusha and met at the Mt. Meru Hotel. It was unusual, made up of thatched cottages. We had a lovely lunch and a briefing meeting. All I can remember is that we were told to be careful of the monkeys. They were most friendly and would enter your room if you left a window open. We took off at once for Lake Manyara National Park.

The hotel was on the rim of the Great Rift Wall. The hot water and lights were unpredictable, but the buffet was excellent. We had chicken, pork, potatoes, gravy, and Indian bread. I had to buy some wine to go with this feast.

The next morning we had a game drive in the park. The lake was gorgeous. It is famous for its spectacular bird life and tree-climbing lions. There were blinds where you could walk to photograph. It was lovely, but there seemed to be a shortage of what it was famous for. As we started to leave the hotel we saw a huge number of large storks perched on the buildings.

We were on our way to Serengeti. The roads were in very bad shape, but we didn't mind. The wildlife made it all worthwhile. The Serengeti was once a lake. Now it is an immense plain caused by a volcanic eruption forming the Ngorongore Caldera millions of years ago. We saw great herds of zebra, wildebeest, and Grant's gazelles. There was one leopard sprawled out on a tree limb. He was partially hidden, making it almost impossible to capture him on film. We passed large pools filled with hippos. Lions were everywhere. They even came walking up close to our vehicles. Many were sprawled out on Kopjes in small groups, napping or staring into space. They were not alarmed by our presence.

This night we stayed in a most unusual lodge built into enormous rocks. Huge boulders formed part of the wall at the dining room entrance. I was astounded by the ingenuity of the architects and builders of this structure. It was quite elaborate.

Two exceptional game drives were planned the next day to follow the paths of the animal migration. One of these lasted four hours. We saw twenty-three lions, many hippos, one leopard, and a variety of birds.

Before leaving for Olduvai Gorge and Ngorongoro Crater, we had one last game drive in the Serengeti. We then went on to the Gorge. It was there, in the late 1950's, that Drs. Mary and Louis Leakey, well-known anthropologists, discovered hominid fossil fragments which they classified as Homo habilis. These were the 1.75 million-year old remains of early man. In 1972, Leakey's son, Richard, found another skull of Homo habilis that is estimated to be two million years old. Homo habilis had an erect posture and human-like hand bones. We saw where the diggings had occurred. The landscape was not attractive.

We moved on towards Ngorongoro National Park. Arriving at the crater's rim, we were told that Ngorongoro was at one time one of the largest volcanic mountains in the world. The top blew off two and one half million years ago. It erupted and collapsed becoming a caldera. The crater is more than 100 square miles with steep sides which create a unique self contained ecosystem. The floor is home to huge herds of plains animals including rhinos, hippos, leopards, lions, and even elephants.

Again, the accommodations were exceptional in the Ngorongoro Safari Lodge.

The next morning we descended the two thousand foot wall into the crater in our four-wheel drive vehicles. This was a full day "game drive." Here, we hit the "jackpot." The number and variety of animals were unbelievable. There was a mother rhino with her baby lying down placidly in the grass. Large flocks of cattle egrets follow the rhinos to seek insects. Two enormous male lions adorned with magnificent manes were sprawled out in a field completely ignoring us. Under one cluster of three trees, seven lions were gathered together. Some were asleep and others were holding their proud heads up looking at us with disdain. A female lion was spotted resting near a pool. Another group of lions was taking advantage of the shade under other trees. One preferred to be in the sun in front of his friends. Several large male lions were truly majestic. Each one was resting alone and apart from all of the others. Each held his gorgeous head high. This was the epitome of aloofness. At one stop we interrupted three females busy eating on the carcass of a gazelle. We came upon a huge male lion with one female. Another female ambled up and went directly to the male and licked his face.

There were scraggly hyenas prowling around in one area. Pools were filled with hippos. Some lay stone still resembling boulders in the water. Others dove under and came up snorting with enormous jaws wide open exhibiting sharp tusk-like teeth in their huge mouths.

Large flocks of flamingoes inhabit Lake Makat. There are many other birds seen there such as sacred ibis, ostrich, kori bustard, Egyptian vultures, the tawny eagle, secretary birds, and marabou stork. This is an ornithologist's paradise.

We had a picnic lunch on the floor of the crater which I shall never forget. As I sat eating a piece of fried chicken breast, a huge black kite bird swooped down and zoomed in on me. He stole the chicken. This is a predatory bird of the hawk family. I was left shaken and hungry as well. The guides were certainly concerned also.

The next morning we had to leave this place of rapture and delight. This place so filled with animals and birds, had surpassing beauty. It was a painful experience to move on. We drove to Mountain Village, a private lodge on a coffee plantation at Lake Duluti. After lunch, a group of us walked around the water's edge along the entirety of the lovely lake. This was a restful respite from all the excitement of the crater. We had charming accommodations.

We moved on rapidly in the morning for the Kilimanjaro International Airport in Arusha. We got a charter flight back to Nairobi. Lunch was at the Safari Park Hotel. We left at once for Nyeri and Mt. Kenya National Park. We were to stay at the Mountain Lodge Tree Hotel on the forested slopes of Mt. Kenya. It was built on high elevation overlooking an animal water hole and salt lick. There were verandahs all along one side of the hotel and photo hides below, where we could view the floodlit water hole and photograph the game as they came to drink. When we retired after dinner, we were told that the hotel personnel would knock on our doors during the night when the animals arrived at the water. This they did numerous times, announcing the animals which were present. "elephants at the water hole," or "wild pigs at the water hole" was to be heard throughout the night, as they knocked on each individual's door.

This was a fascinating place. We saw seventeen elephants in the morning coming to drink and bathe. There was a group of wild pigs. Three Cape buffalo appeared and seven waterbuck. From the verandahs up high one could watch and photograph under ideal conditions. I was not ready to leave, but we had to depart for Nanyuki and the luxurious Mt. Kenya Safari Club, located in the shadow of Mt. Kenya. This place was founded by the late actor, William Holden.

Crossing the equator on our way, we arrived in time for a smörgâsbord luncheon. I had a lovely cabin with fireplace and flowers all to myself. This place was sumptuous. Men were required to wear jackets and ties to dinner and the ladies to dress accordingly.

There was plenty to see wandering over the spacious, beautifully landscaped grounds with an abundance of flowers. There was a museum. They had in captivity a miniature antelope, the Suni. It was about the size of a big jack rabbit and absolutely adorable. There were numerous peacocks strolling around or perched on the porch railings. Several Crowned Cranes appeared sporting their magnificent headdress.

After only one night, we were off again for Lake Nakuru and Lake Naivasha. The pace and variety on this tour was unbelievable. They truly tried to take us and show us as much as was humanly possible within the time limits. I was completely overwhelmed by the beauty of the different landscapes and the quantity of animals we saw on the frequent game drives.

On the way, we took a side trip to see a large waterfall cascading down through the dense green foliage of many trees. We finally entered the Great Rift Valley. It is twenty-five miles across and six thousand miles long, the same distance as from the Red Sea to Mozambique. Lake Nakuru is a fresh water lake which has a large population of flamingos, pelicans, and storks. There is a sanctuary for the endangered black rhino. There is an interesting distinction between the white rhino and the black rhino. The white are grazers with wide lips. The black are browsers with pointed lips. The upper lip extends in a trunk-like fashion. It is used to pull out wild herbs and seedlings, or to tear off leaves from bushes or low trees. They are victims of poachers seeking the horns for medicinal purposes or for making the handles of daggers for the men of Yemen.

We had lunch overlooking the lake and continued on to Lake Naivasha Country Club to spend the night. The rooms were precious. The next morning, I walked down to the lovely lake to take pictures of the birds and boats. There was a structure built out in the water near the shore. It had a roof where large clusters of birds gathered together to take a break. We weren't about to take a break. After breakfast, we departed across the valley for the Masai Mara Game Reserve—Northern Serengeti. This place was loaded with elephants, lions, leopards, buffalo, rhinos and thousands of other plains animals. There were piles of hippos stacked on each other in the Mara River. We saw thirteen lions stalking three cape buffalo. There were hyena puppies on view. We stopped for lunch at the Keekorok Lodge and the continued our game drive. It was spectacular. We ended up at the Mara Serena Lodge on a ridge overlooking the escarpment. We had one more day with two full game drives and another night at the lodge. In the morning there was another drive at dawn. We encountered cheetahs and leopards.

Our time was running out. We had to drive back to Nairobi for a stay in a dayroom at the Safari Park Hotel while waiting for our KLM flight to Amsterdam, and then on to New York.

The sadness on departing Africa was beyond all description. I was torn up emotionally. All I could think about was that I had to return. I did, the next year. Meanwhile my heart ached for Africa and still does.

The Frivolous Fanatical Fling, 1992-1993

For several years now, where I was teaching, some of my superiors seemed determined to force me into retirement. This was a very unpleasant and painful period. I think the reasons were that I was at top salary and they used my age as a factor. I was only sixty-nine and never felt more energetic, as I dearly loved my students. It was as if they wanted to put the clamps on me, even having one administrator pop into my classes regularly to observe. This did not bother me, but it got to be so ridiculous that my students would comment saying: "What is she doing here again?" It was embarrassing and at times, distracting. I hung on until the end. I was praised highly by a principal from another school when I underwent four observations from four different schools. It seemed as if they were not going to give up until I was gone. Meanwhile, I applied for twenty-one hours in E.S.L. (English Second Language) training at the Baptist College in Phoenix. I was accepted and attended these classes in the evenings after teaching all day. This course cost the district about three thousand dollars. I completed it and became certified as an E.S.L. teacher. I was grateful for this experience and opportunity. Nevertheless, I had to resign in 1993. Knowing I was nearing the end of my monetary means, I went into a state of frenzied activity. I took every Arizona Outdoor and Travel Club trip I could.

In June, 1992, after my return from Africa, I went to Los Cabos, Mexico for ten days. I suffered a gastrointestinal hemorrhage in November and was in the hospital taking blood transfusions. I left the hospital and went back to teach three days before Thanksgiving break. My daughter and I then joined the Arizona Outdoor and Travel Club's annual trip to San Carlos, Mexico for Thanksgiving. It was a nice experience. We were treated to a festive Thanksgiving dinner. I took my daughter on a deep-sea fishing excursion. We did not have a catch, but dined on the fish others had caught and cooked right on the boat. We boated all around the Sea of Cortez. We went down by bus from Phoenix and returned by bus.

Christmas brought out the wanderlust in me again. I headed for Cozumel, Mexico. I had been here before and found it to be very relaxing, just taking in the sun and doing a little snorkeling.

1993—Last Year to Teach

I already had another trip planned to go to Africa in September, but I had to try everything else until that glorious moment arrived. In February, I went on a horseback riding trip with the Arizona Outdoor and Travel Club in the Superstition Mountains near Phoenix. It turned out to be a six-hour ride and I had not been on a horse for six years.

It was a very rugged trail with beautiful scenery. I must say I enjoyed it thoroughly until I tried to get off of the horse. That was sheer agony. Being arthritic, both knees were so painful that I could hardly walk over to a pick-up truck to lean against. I had a gentle beautiful horse with blue eyes. I had asked someone to take a picture of me before I climbed down. I remarked that I needed this picture to remind me never to try this again.

In March there was another trip with the club to Payson, Arizona. We hiked through the pines and had a lunch prepared by a member who lived in that area. This was a great contrast to the horseback trip.

For Spring Break in 1993, I went back to Cozumel, Mexico for a week. This was a "get a tan" relaxation period. In April, there was a four-wheel trip to Coke Ovens and Rug Mountain. That was a weekend trip and we camped out. That was my passion, setting up my tent and cooking out. On that trip we drove out to and around the copper mining country of Arizona. The old coke ovens were used in the mining operation some time ago. They are no longer in use. We had an unbelievable experience on that trip. We had to climb what they called Rug Mountain. The road was bad, being steep and narrow. Someone in the past had laid down rugs on the road's surface for one stretch so that the vehicles could get traction. This was an astounding sight to see all the different colors and patterns of rugs covering the road. Even with the rugs, some cars had a rough time getting up the hill. One person even broke down. We all proceeded on our way and stopped for dinner. Everyone sat on a curb and waited hours for our friend to be rescued. We found someone in the small town to go back and bring the vehicle out. It was late in the night when we finally made our way back to Phoenix.

The next month came a trip with the club to Hualapi Indian Reservation in the northwest corner of Arizona. This area adjoins a section of Grand Canyon National Park. It was another weekend campout with pleasant scenery in contrast to the desert near Phoenix. However, nothing spectacular or out of the ordinary occurred. I reveled in setting up my small quaint tent which had been used on field trips by an oil company in Peru. I also made a big deal over my cooking on the unstable wobbly little propane stove. There was always a T-bone steak, mushrooms, and a fresh vegetable, such as broccoli. This was sumptuous as far as I was concerned. I could live like this forever. How could so little make me so happy? It was a glorious weekend.

We squeezed in one more weekend trip to cabins near Payson, Arizona. It was a camp of sorts. Each person prepared his own food in a mess hall building near the cabins. There was one strange thing on this sojourn. We found that the cabins were already occupied by many small mice. This was disconcerting to say the least. They came alive at night. This was enough to make me hesitate to get out of bed in the middle of the night for a restroom visit. I tried to talk myself out of it. I was extremely uncomfortable because at that time the Hanta Virus was appearing in the state. Several people had lost their lives after being infected. The virus is carried by mice. It was just another experience! Each one of these trips certainly had its own peculiarity, which made it impossible to forget.

Glacier National Park—July 1993

Now came the big one. A trip to Glacier and Waterton Lakes National Parks was on the agenda. We flew from Phoenix to Missoula, Montana. Our first night was spent in a very nice motel on a raging river. We had dinner that night overlooking the river. We got into our vehicles the next day and started the lengthy drive. We passed through lovely countryside with numerous ranches. Eventually, we reached mountains with patches of snow. There were bright yellow flowered meadows caressing the base of the mountains. Icy cold streams abounded. Pure white mountain goats were found nestled in the lush green growth.

The geology of this area is something to ponder. It has been suggested that it might be more appropriate if the Glacier Park entrance signs welcomed you to Glaciated National Park. The present name of the park refers not so much to glaciers existing today, but to the long past Ice Age glaciers which shaped the marvelous scenery of Glacier and Waterton. Over the past two million years huge glaciers carved the mountains and valleys we see today. The force of these gigantic glaciers is witnessed in today's landscape.

About 60 to 170 million years ago, there was a collision of the Pacific oceanic plate with the North American continental plate. This caused a folding, buckling, and breaking of rock layers. This steady pressure thrust up and pushed eastward huge slabs which eventually became the Rocky Mountains, when things calmed down.

About two million years ago, a drastic cooling global climate brought on the Ice Age. This is a phenomenon which might very well be welcomed today, considering the dreadful effects of our present day warming trend. Massive glaciers formed in the mountains and filled the valleys. These glaciers advanced and retreated from time to time as the temperatures fluctuated. During this process, the sculpturing of the landscape took place.

Ten to twelve thousand years ago the huge Ice Age glaciers retreated and melted away when the climate warmed. We are now left with the magnificent scenery of Glacier and Waterton Lakes National Parks. Plants and animals came back to inhabit the valleys and mountains.

Only fifty or so small glaciers, formed only 5000 years ago, exist in Glacier National Park today. There are no active glaciers in Waterton Lakes National Park. The existing glaciers have been shrinking for the last one hundred years. No one knows their future. In my opinion, our present day fears of global warming are certainly justified. I can see no hope of ever seeing the massive glaciers form again. I see no prospect of another Ice Age, which gave birth to the powerful gifted glacial carvers of the past.

We drove on toward a place called Rising Sun, buying and eating huge bags of beautiful cherries, along the way. We arrived at Lake McDonald. We hiked around the lake and to the falls. Lunch was our leftover steak and chips from the night before. We went on to our camping spot on St. Mary Lake, a slender "snaking" lake. Bright red mountains loomed up across the lake. Numerous deer ambled along the shore stepping into the water to drink now and then.

We had the option of setting up our tents or renting one of the cabins. The grounds were very wet and bears were known to drop in. I chickened out. Another lady and I rented a cabin. We ate in the main building where there was a restaurant. The rest of the gang visited us to take showers in our cabin.

After a church service on Sunday, several of us took a boat ride. We traveled on the lake past small islands, viewing the surrounding low mountains with patches of snow. We landed at one spot and took a hike along the water and into the forest. Before boarding our boat, we walked to Bering Falls. This was a magnificent waterfall. It cascaded down abruptly at several levels, foaming at the base.

The next day, the whole group hiked up to Hidden Lake. There were steps made from large wooden planks going up the mountain to this lake. It resembled a boardwalk. I was slower than the rest of the group and found myself climbing up these endless planks all alone. I met a friendly lady who was coming down. She told me about the large group of white mountain goats at the top near Hidden Lake. This information spurred me on. I also learned that a bear had been had been on this trail the day before. This news almost caused me to turn around. I put aside my cowardly thoughts and trudged on. When I finally arrived at the top, everyone clapped and cheered. They insisted on taking a picture of me at the top. The lake was indeed hidden. It was small but lovely. All around were white goats, some munching on the grass and others lounging peacefully. It was worth the difficult climb.

Everyone started back down. I ambled and photographed the little marmots. I encountered several people along the way and had to visit. One was a ranger. We discussed the bear situation. The boardwalk was one and one half miles one way. In the distance, were mountains, occasional peaks, and cones with patches of snow. Again, I was the last to arrive at the bottom. Here the leader was anxiously waiting for me. I detected a slight annoyance for my holding up the group, but I greeted him cheerfully. On the way back to the lodging, we stopped at a spectacular lookout to take pictures. This was Logan Pass, which straddles the Continental Divide.

The next day we drove to the Many Glacier Hotel for lunch. We were on our way to Grinnell Glacier which is one of the fifty small remote glaciers formed only about five thousand years ago. We took a tour boat with a guide along Swift current and Josephine lakes. We got on the trail which led us to the Grinnell Lake and Glacier. We had to cross a swinging plank bridge. It was extremely unstable and tricky to walk across. There were many marmots popping out here and there. After investigating the lake and glacier, we had to tackle the swinging bridge again, then take another trail to Hidden Falls. These falls and lakes were really "hidden," only accessible by trails.

Now we were to start the long five hundred mile drive to Banff via Waterton Lakes. We came upon the Prince of Wales Hotel overlooking Waterton Lake. From a distance, as we approached, it had the appearance of a "gingerbread" edifice. It was charming, painted white with red and royal blue trim. Massive picture windows provided a view of the lake. This seven story hotel with eighty-one rooms was built in 1927 by the Great Northern Railway. At one time, it was nearly blown to pieces by high winds. It withstood the weather. Now it appears like a crown jewel to the seven-mile long string of mountains that surround the lake. It was named for Great Britain's King Edward VIII, the Prince of Wales. We had several hours to stroll around the interior and the grounds.

On we went. The terrain was magnificent with mountains and lakes. We had a most unusual brief stopover at a town called Frank. This was a mining town near Turtle Mountain. In the early morning darkness of April 29, 1903, at ten minutes after four, a gigantic wedge of limestone, 800 meters across, 140 meters deep, and 550 meters high, crashed down from Turtle Mountain onto the town of Frank. Eighty-two million tons of rock swept across Crowsnest Valley in about one hundred seconds. The rock slide took sixty-eight lives, destroyed the town, and buried the rail lines as well as the entire mine plant.

The miners, who were working inside the mountain at the time managed to dig their way out only to be confronted with the devastation of the town. The mine did reopen for awhile, but the original town could not recover. It was moved to its present location. It seems that this geological event has not been explained to this day.

Arriving at Banff, completely exhausted, we went to a hostel which was to be our base of operations. We had a day to explore the town, the lake, and take the gondola ride.

The next few days were spent visiting Lake Louise, with its monstrous chateau, and the Athabasca Glacier. We shared Lake Louise with large groups of tourists from Japan. We arrived at the glacier and spent considerable time hiking along its base. We found our way to Athabasca Falls and Takkakaw Falls. I captured the beauty of these falls with my camera.

Back in Banff we managed to squeeze in one evening at a chamber music concert. Then it was time to start our long drive back to pick up our flight back to Arizona.

Twenty-six Day Custom Kenya-Zimbabwe Safari September 1993

I was off again for Africa. I didn't get off to a very good start. There was a long delay in Phoenix to get to Los Angeles to catch my American Airlines flight to London. After arriving in London in the morning, I had to wait until 8:15 P.M. for the overnight Kenya Airways flight to Nairobi. I didn't even try to go into London. I sat in the airport, jostling my luggage and two new cameras, until that night. It was not a pleasant experience. I was exhausted before I even got to Kenya. Then there was no representative to meet me in Nairobi. I was beginning to wonder if all of these happenings were ominous. I took a taxi to the hotel where I was supposed to have reservations. I called the local travel agent. He finally showed up full of apologies. He moved me to a different hotel and even carried my beat-up suitcase into the lobby himself. He tried to make amends by arranging for a driver to take me to the Karen Blixen home and the Giraffe Center. He threw in the Animal Orphanage. I had been to these places on my first trip to Africa. I was not impressed nor very receptive after all I had been through.

The next day I was taken to the Wilson Airport for the light aircraft flight to Samburu, in the dry northern bush country. This was the first of the three camps I was to stay in, Larsen's Camp, located on the Ewaso Ngiro River. It was very comfortable, in fact luxurious. Each tent was named after a bird. I had my own little cool green tent named Curlews. There were twin beds and a separate bathroom. The rugs were especially woven for the camp. There were stairs leading up to the porch with chairs. A vervet monkey joined me on the porch one day and sat up on the back of one of the chairs for me to take his picture. Later, other monkeys came up and investigated my purse.

Meals were served from a large patio with barbecue, overlooking the river. Many birds of every kind were in this area. We had lunch there. The food was superb. They served marinated lamb charcoal broiled, potatoes, pepper gravy, spinach, and a pastry in the shape of a swan.

We took our first wildlife drive. We saw groups of Beisa oryx and Fringedear oryx, a cheetah with a recent antelope kill, and a small female lion resting in the shade of a tree. Another female was drinking from a pool nearby where a small bird was wading. A group of Reticulated giraffes stretched their necks into the trees. The colors and patterns of these animals were exquisite. I got a perfect shot of the giraffes' bodies and legs, but no heads. This is not exactly good photography.

We saw several of my favorite little antelope, the gerenuk. They are exquisite with long legs and elongated necks. They stand up on their hind legs and place their forelegs against the bush they are feeding on. I wanted to take one home with me. Then two mundane Mourning doves posed. This picture turned out very well and could have been taken in my backyard at home.

We encountered a large group of elephants. Two males got into a serious sparring match right next to our vehicle. They were very serious, verging on violence, in this confrontation. Our driver was anxious to get out of there. We drove off quickly and ran into a family of baboons with their colorful posteriors. The little ones were romping about and wrestling on the ground.

So what's for dinner at a remote camp in Africa? Sherry, chicken bouillon, veal, potatoes, and broiled tomatoes.

On our second day, the abundance and variety of animals was again overwhelming. We found two gorgeous cheetahs resting near the foot of a tree. The tree had only a spray of black limbs thrusting forth from its thick dark trunk. There were no leaves. It made a perfect backdrop. The animals were nestled in among thick wispy clumps of light beige-colored grass. One of them raised his lovely head with the black tear lines running down his cheeks from his eyes. The other one continued to snooze, partially hidden.

A spindly-legged, long-necked gerenuk browsed placidly. Two others stood and reached into the bushes. A large family of elephants gathered on the riverbank. Only one was wading in the water. A large female lion dozed with eyes closed, then opened her eyes slightly to be photographed. Four oryx, three giraffes, and a small wart hog gathered in an area, each one ignoring the others as they went about eating. There were no dangers or predators, only the vehicles carrying us. We did not concern the animals.

On an early morning drive, we saw eight lions at one place and a great variety of birds. A cheetah was eating a baby zebra. The mother was standing over in the field, looking very sad and forlorn, completely helpless.

We passed a huge red termite hill stacked up at the base of an elegant Acacia tree. It extended up quite high into the lower limbs. It looked like the tree was growing up out of a pile of red sand. I assume this is symbiotic relationship. The tree looked healthy. On one free limb there was suspended a Weaver's nest, the typical meticulously constructed ball with a small hole for an entrance. This is a finch-like bird native to Africa. The nest hung all alone, which I thought was strange. The ones I had seen before were in large groups on the same tree.

Going back to the river we saw four huge yellow-billed storks wading and a lovely vervet monkey peering out from the bushes. I walked from the restaurant along the river and photographed an alligator.

We watched a mother lion carrying her cub in her mouth across the river. It was a fantastic picture. I was so excited that I forgot to use the zoom.

We spent three nights at the Larsen's camp in Samburu. There were three game drives each day. On the day of our departure, we had an early morning drive before breakfast. Then we departed from the Samburu Airstrip in a small plane headed for Nairobi. On arrival, I was taken to the famous Carnivore Restaurant for lunch. Here they serve every imaginable kind of wild game such as wildebeest and alligator. Since I was on the custom tour, I was seated all alone in the restaurant. The driver was not allowed to join me. I was not very happy. Leaving the restaurant, I looked up as I climbed into the waiting vehicle and saw Paul, one of my drivers on my first trip to Africa the year before. I was ecstatic and I wanted to visit with him, but we had to move on to the second camp. We drove almost three hours. We paused at a high point overlooking the Great Rift Valley, the world's largest fault. There were some beautiful white sheepskins on display. I had to buy one, never thinking about the trouble or inconvenience of carrying it around for the rest of the tour.

My driver took me to an African crafts shop where a large number of shields, highly decorated battle shields, were on display. I resisted the temptation. Then we went to observe a spot where stacks of wood were being processed for the fabulous wood carvers to work on.

Eventually, we arrived at Delamere's Camp in the Soysambu Wildlife Sanctuary. The camp tents overlooked the alkaline Lake Elmenteita. This was a bird sanctuary. Hundreds of pink flamingos clustered at the edge of the lake. We drove up to the escarpment with a beautiful view of the lake and were served cocktails and hors d'oeuvres while we watched the brilliant sunset.

This turned out to be quite a social gathering. I tried to take pictures with my new Minolta. Being more accurate and informed than I, the camera refused to take the pictures. I struggled. I had not learned how to put on manual focus yet. This was a frustrating experience.

We went back down to the luxurious lodge for dinner. There was an amusing incident at dinner. I was trying to visit with a lady who only spoke French. In desperation, I asked a young girl near me if she spoke French. She said, "Yes." I asked her to speak to the lady and she said, "Sure, I will. She's my mother."

Then came a night drive from nine until eleven. We viewed the aardvark, mongoose, and the African hare, which were numerous. The aardvark, also called the ant bear, was a grotesque animal. It had an elongated snout, long pointed ears, and a tail which was thick at the base, but tapered to a point. It has strong digging claws. It feeds on ants and termites which it captures with its long viscid tongue. It is strictly nocturnal and solitary, and seldom seen. The African hare is also solitary and nocturnal. It has long ears and legs. The hare and the mongoose were not that exciting to see.

Soon we did encounter some excitement. There was a group of water buffalo, which can be extremely fierce. We picked them up with the lights of the vehicle, then we stalled out. There were a few uneasy moments. We finally got the engine started. The animals reacted in an unfriendly manner. I believe they thought it was too late in the night for visitors.

The next morning, before breakfast, there was a long walk with a young man who was an ornithologist. His name was Willis. I have been corresponding with him ever since this encounter. He was also an artist and a photographer. He has sent me an exquisite watercolor of an African bird and several of his photos.

After breakfast, we were off again on a two and one half hours drive around the lake, visiting the bird watching blinds. We passed a rustic tree house, complete with stairway and thatched roof. It had to be investigated by our climbing up into the interior. It did not seem to be occupied and was in ill repair.

We had another "sunset rendezvous." I continued to persuade my camera and to utter an occasional swear word at its obstinacy. There was a repeat performance, down for dinner and off for a night drive. This was not at all unusual nor too interesting, merely a repeat of the night before as far as the viewing of the animals was concerned.

On my last day, another guide named Paul drove me to Lake Nakuru. We spent the whole day together. We drove through a forest before arriving at the edge of the lake. Many warthogs, impala and waterbuck were postured in the pasture around the lake. I took picture after picture. At the edge of the lake there were thousands of the greater and lesser flamingos. The greater bird is much larger and not as colorful as the "lesser." It seems strange to me that these birds frequent the extremely alkaline lakes in such great numbers. There were also white pelicans and geese.

After spending much time in this area near the lake, we drove to a high lookout to view the lake with the lovely mountains in the background, bordering the lake. Then there was the descent to the other side of the lake at the base of the mountains. Two huge buffalo were resting among the trees. Many giraffes were ambling among the trees, posing in various positions. I handed my video camera to Paul while I clicked away on the Minolta. My favorite Secretary bird appeared. This is a large pale gray, long-legged bird with black flight feathers and tibia and long central tail feathers. It has conspicuous crest feathers which resemble a halo. It has orange around the eyes with a patch of bright yellow near its beak. It feeds on snakes and other reptiles. It is enchanting, and an ideal subject for a watercolor which I have yet to do.

After a late lunch, Paul met me again on the grounds for a Botany session. He identified and provided information, such as medicinal benefits, about each plant growing around the premises. He knew all of the Latin names. I took notes vigorously. As I look over these notes I am amused. I might as well pass on some of this vital information. Any reader who is a botanist can check it out for veracity.

Aloe *senetos* is for colds, wounds, and Malaria. Aloe *griminicora* juice is used for colds and burns. The jelly can be put in hot water to drink. He claimed that a rust-colored aloe can be used as a catalyst to make beer. You can cook it in hot water with honey and in two to three days you have beer. Its juice is an antibiotic and the flower is eaten by the sunbird. The Portoreca dedrocadra is a poisonous plant. Other animals eating it will die, but the small Dikdik antelope and the

Eland can eat it without a problem. The Codia ovaris, the sandpaper tree, is used to make a walking stick. You sand it with the leaf of the tree, put it in mud one week, and it comes out a nice black finish. Osimum suave smells like mint. It is a mosquito repellent, and controls termites. Ruz naturense has a fruit edible for monkeys, birds, bats, and young boys. The bark can be cooked and taken as a tea or eaten as porridge. It kills worms, including the pin worm. Gemirea simmeres is eaten by giraffe, antelope, and birds. The Maetina senegalalenses has roots which can be used for a backache. You cook it and drink it as a tea. The bark can be dried, made into a powder, and used on wounds. Aloe *kedodenses* is used for malaria, wounds, sunburn, and fire burns. One teaspoon is the dosage.

It was time to say goodbye to my dear friends Willis, Paul, and George. I brought the dress I had made from material I bought in Kenya previously along with my Indian jewelry from Arizona to show them.

The next morning, coffee was brought to the tent. I bathed, washed my hair, and packed up. I filmed all of the tent facilities and staff. It was time to head for Nairobi. We had to take a private charter plane to the Masai Mara National Reserve where our third camp. the Mara River Camp, was located. Nairobi was terribly crowded, but the jacaranda and bougainvillea were beautiful. There was a traffic jam to get to the airport. We arrived in Masai Mara late in the afternoon, and drove ten kilometers across the plains loaded with zebras, wildebeest, and warthogs. Thompson's gazelles and Topi were numerous. The Masai villages with their inhabitants were all around us. It was extremely picturesque.

The camp was right on the Mara River. In front of my tent, there was a large hill rising up, covered with a mass of large trees. I looked up to see three huge baboons running around in the forest. A little gray and white kitten befriended me. She had been in my tent, jumping up on the bedside table and into the laundry basket. Then she rested on one of the chairs on the porch with me.

I heard the hippos in the river right in front of the tent. One of them came up on the bank, but I failed to get his picture. The river was full of hippos. Some were in the water and many were clumped together on a sandbar taking in the sun.

A huge log fire was built in a pit in front of the restaurant overlooking the river. Our dinner consisted of pork chops, applesauce, potatoes, gravy, and green beans. It was excellent.

The next day was full of wildlife runs. We left at seven o'clock. Benjamin was our guide and Edwin the ornithologist. We left the River Mara and came up on a wide plain with the escarpment in the background. Masai huts with their fenced in cattle were everywhere. They are an extremely colorful people. The men and the little boys were all wrapped up in brightly colored panels of cloth. I had made my dress from one of these panels. They herd the goats and cattle across this vast expanse. I was told that the Cape buffalo kill more Masai than does any other wild animal.

Out on the plains there were hundreds of wildebeest, zebras, Topi, warthogs, and the Thomson's gazelles, with their black tails wagging. We encountered two gorgeous lions, a male and female. There were groups of black buffalo behind a large white tree trunk, which created a contrasting composition for a picture. I took much video to show the massive groups of animals moving around and the great quantity of vultures hovering about, ready to finish off every particle of a kill. The Secretary birds strutted among the zebra and wildebeest.

In a grove of trees, stood a magnificent male elephant, six females, and several babies. They moved around a lot, curling up their trunks while picking up food.

We parked on a hill by the River Mara. There were stacks of hippos. At the same spot, I got a picture of a huge crocodile lying on a sandbar with his mouth wide open. The video camera never stopped.

In the afternoon we were off again. We passed a flock of chestnut-colored sand grouse with the white streak around their eyes. They resemble the dove. Very near were fifteen elephants with their four young ones. Walking along with them was an ostrich. Later, we saw five huge ostrich eggs lying in a depression on the ground, unguarded. Four lion mothers with their seven cubs were secluded in the thick bushes. They didn't want to be photographed. In the distance, there were hundreds of wildebeest walking across the plains in a perfect line, which appeared to have no beginning and no end. It looked like a follow-the-leader procession. They were silhouetted against the sky. The was no end to the quantity and variety of animals, especially around a water hole where we paused for some time. Many magically marked zebra were drinking at the pools while hyenas lurked a short distance away.

The glorious peak of excitement, reaching a crescendo, was when we came upon a large mother cheetah with her three cubs beneath a tree. This turned out to be the ultimate culmination. They were meticulously tearing apart and eating a recently captured Thomson's Gazelle. The driver and I were completely captivated to the point of being mesmerized. We could not leave. The vehicle was parked just a few feet away from the animals. We spent many minutes there, filming frantically with both cameras.

The driver filled me in with some facts: the cheetah has very good eyesight, with binocular vision like the human, but cannot see color. Most animals don't see color, except for the giraffe. The cheetah has spots where the leopard has four to five spots grouped into what is called a rosette. It has the shape of a greyhound with long slender legs, a black tear mark from the eye to the mouth, a small head, and is the most unsuccessful carnivore. There are four to five young in a litter, but there is a high mortality rate with only about two surviving. There are many rocks in the area it inhabits and in which it is forced to hunt. Here its feet can be injured or a leg broken. Then he will die, not being able to forage or run. Their numbers are declining. In Asia and India they have been tamed in the same way as falcons, and have been used in hunting. Some were even pets.

We lingered a long time. We discovered that the gazelle had been pregnant. We watched the three cubs demolishing the body and one cub was eating the placenta. The mother licked the blood from each cub's mouth from time to time. At first, the mother's large body and the three cubs were huddled close to the carcass, eating. Then the mother, satiated, moved away and sprawled out to rest. One or two of the cubs continued to work vigorously to satisfy their hunger. This was truly an enchanting drama being enacted before our eyes.

After an early morning drive the next day, I flew to Nairobi where I spent the night. The following morning, I was driven to the Amboseli Lodge in Amboseli National Park where I was booked for two nights. The lodge overlooks Mt. Kilimanjaro, Africa's highest peak at 19,340 feet. I had missed this spectacle on my first trip to Africa because of cloud cover.

I was taken out immediately on an afternoon drive, across the grassy swampland. Mt. Kilimanjaro served as a backdrop for the hundreds of elephants, zebras, and wildebeest ambling about this massive plain. My driver took me to a lookout mountain rising above the plains. We climbed up many steps to the top. Here I took panoramic views of the Great Rift Valley dotted with wildlife. Dust devils danced into view from time to time.

We came down to drive among the elephants and zero in on close-up views. We were right among these massive majestic creatures. They have a close knit family and lovingly nurture the baby elephants. It's true that the male is absent most of the time, but it is touching to see how the mother elephant and the other females care for the young. Some of these huge animals were covered with blotches of mud from the waters. You can even see the water line on some. Many of the babies were nursing.

Returning to the lodge, we had a flat tire. We waited for another vehicle. At last, one passed by with a tire. Francis, my driver changed it and we headed back to the lodge.

We left again in the late afternoon to photograph the sunset and Mt. Kilimanjaro. At one point, I captured a brilliant rainbow dropping down to the earth from a flock of white fluffy clouds with dark streaks on their underside.

Our vehicle stalled right in the middle of a herd of elephants. We couldn't get it started. We had to wait until the animals passed in front of us, then finally got the engine running. Earlier, we had met a band of Masai children in the middle of the road. I gave them gum, candy, and money. Then I photographed them.

Early the next morning, Francis and I started on a drive before breakfast. He seemed preoccupied. He was having a battery problem and had to pick someone up at the airport, so we went to look for hippos. We found a Masai man standing in the middle of the swamp with the elephants and hippos all around him. I persuaded him to get into the vehicle with us so we could drive him to a safer place.

There was one more drive before we had to fly to Nairobi. We found a lone black female rhino. She was called a browser because of the pointed lips she uses to seek food. The white rhino has a square lip and is called a grazer. We ran into a mother hyena with her cubs. Then we had the unbelievable good fortune to find another gorgeous cheetah. She was all alone, tearing apart and gnawing on a small blood-spattered gazelle. She ate for awhile, and then would pick up the carcass. She would carry it and drop it at another spot. In one photo I have of her, she is majestically posing with the mangled gazelle lying between her two front feet. She finally abandoned it and lay down on a knoll, completely relaxed. She looked across the plains, then turned her head and stared directly at us. The remains of her feast lay near her back feet.

She changed her position again, in an almost restless manner. My last two pictures show her reclining with her body lying on the upward slope of the kopje, her body taking the same form as the mound. Her majestic magnificent head was in posed profile displaying the dark black tear marks running from her eye down her cheek into the lower jaw.

The display was not over. Farther on there appeared a huge wart hog with an enormous head. He was eating peacefully, ignoring us. I wondered why God made this animal so grotesquely ugly.

After my flight to Nairobi, a guide took me to the Bomas. There was a display of African music and dance. There were also groups of typical huts of the various African tribes which we could examine. Each dwelling had its distinctive features. In front of each one, the crafts and objects of interest were spread out for the tourist to purchase. My defense was weakened. I bought a drum, a shell, a carved fish, and a decorative carved frog. The fish and frog were from stone.

They were well done, and actually exquisite in design. One vendor had the same name as I, Margaret. This seemed to bond us. She gave me a colorful necklace of seeds and pods. I still wear it almost every day with my silver chains.

I was scheduled to take the overnight train to Mombasa that night. There was a train wreck, so I was grounded in the hotel with no television nor air-conditioning. It was very quiet. I enjoyed the peace.

During this delay I had a whole day to catch my breath. I visited a camera shop to find out why I was having so much trouble with my camera. The owner of the shop checked it out and predicted it would have to go back to the factory. He was right.

It was a long wait for the train, which was leaving that night. I sat in the lobby and stared into space. While sitting there, in a semi-trance, a group of eighty soldiers from India walked in. They were very handsome in their uniforms and blue berets. Several were wearing blue turbans twisted around their heads. They were on their way to the peacekeeping in Somalia. It made me sad. I felt more than a twinge of guilt for spending so much money on my African spree when they were sacrificing their lives, perhaps. I said a prayer: "Dear Lord, forgive me."

My driver finally arrived. I was surprised to see an American couple in the car, headed for the train I was taking. They were from Dana Pt., California. One of my dear friends in Phoenix was from this same place. What a coincidence!

We boarded the train. I had a stateroom all to myself, I got lucky. The food was barely edible. I slept longer and better than I anticipated on this vintage train. When I had to go to the restroom, however, I was in for a huge surprise and an impossible challenge. There was only a large slab of cement on the floor with a hole in the center. I had to perch myself above the hole to evacuate.

I assumed that this was not a major problem for the male passengers. However, it proved to be an extremely difficult task, literally a strategic maneuver for me on the lurching train.

The luxury hotel, surrounded by the peculiarly beautiful baobab trees, was a welcome haven. My guide picked me up for a city tour.

The city was full of Muslims and mosques. I had the same uncomfortable feelings I had experienced while in Morocco. I felt ashamed of myself for verging on prejudicial feelings. Salim, my guide, was kind and accommodating. He was proud of his city. I tried to appear enthusiastic.

I was up early the next morning preparing to go to the Mombasa airport to catch a plane for the Island of Lamu. We stopped at Malindi, then went on to Manda Island. There we crossed over by boat to Lamu. This island community is a traditional Arab town. It is very old with Arabic architecture apparent at every corner. It is ninety percent Muslim. There were narrow alleys where many donkey carts passed, transporting goods. There is only one car on the island. Open sewers and the dung of burros was everywhere.

I wandered through the streets for several hours, stepping over the dung. I admired the fascinating buildings, the small shops, and the minarets and cupolas of the central Mosque. Colorful fishing boats rested on the waterfront. The men were wearing skirts and the women were dressed entirely in black garb with black scarves covering their heads and part of their faces. We were limited as to how much we could do or see during our short visit. It was a charming transcendental experience, transporting me back in time. After lunch, it was time to climb into the boat for Manda Island where our plane was waiting to take us back to Mombasa.

Early in the morning, I took a long walk on the beach looking for shells. I passed by a pipe draining raw sewage into the ocean right in front of my lavish hotel. The beach had an unpleasant odor. I was glad that I had not had time to go swimming.

Very soon Salim showed up. I was off for the airport for a flight to Nairobi, where I would make an afternoon connection with the Air Zimbabwe flight to Harare. Another disappointment was awaiting me. My agent did not show up to help me with my luggage and customs. This was the same man who failed to meet me when I first arrived in Nairobi. I could not believe it. A stranger, named Harrison, from another tourist company helped me. Next time I shall use his company.

It couldn't happen three times, but it did. No one met me at Harare. This was making it an impossibility to ever recommend my tour company.

There we were at the deluxe Meikles Hotel, according to my agenda. It took a long time to check in as there was a huge crowd in the lobby. I was very self-conscious and embarrassed carrying my patched up suitcase and my large white plastic bag tied with a knot at the top which held my sheepskin. I was uncomfortable to the point of trying to hide behind any available pillar. Soon, but not too soon, a lovely dinner with wine and music compensated. I had oysters from South Africa and passed up a beef fillet for fish soup which had no fish. I do remember the delicious Indian bread they served. I was almost too tired to eat.

That was only a one night stand. I was up early to catch the plane for Bulawayo. I had a few problems getting a car to the airport so early in the morning. By now, I was beginning to be suspicious about the efficiency of the Masai Mara. Again we found rhinos, impalas, waterbucks, and warthogs. Suffering from fatigue and with my camera not functioning, I was slightly disheartened. I managed to climb up unto an outlook platform. All we saw for the physical exertion were many lizards and shrew. We returned to the camp and I climbed up into the lounge and restaurant for my last pleasant dinner and evening here.

On Sunday it was time to leave. There was no church. Instead, I talked to Althea, the wife of the owner, over breakfast on the patio-like ledge of the restaurant. We discussed religion and the born-again Christian beliefs. It was peaceful. We overlooked the huge boulders. Her husband appeared at the last moment with a neat box. He had packed my sheepskin so that I would never be embarrassed again walking into a hotel lobby with the white plastic bag. I asked him how he had managed to get my big thick white sheepskin into such a small box. He said that he had cut it into pieces. I gasped and then realized he was teasing me. We had a good laugh and I drove off toward the airport at Bulawayo. I waved to Althea with tears in my eyes.

I caught my flight to Harare and on we went to Victoria Falls. I was met and taken to the historic Victoria Falls Hotel. This is a lovely hotel with a fabulous history, as interesting as the story of the falls.

Even though the Victoria Falls had existed for millions of years, The outside world did not know of them until David Livingston happened upon them in 1855. They became a world-wide tourist attraction when the railroad heading north to Cairo was built in 1904.

With the coming of the railroad, materials for the construction of the first Victoria Falls Hotel arrived and construction was underway. The hotel opened in June, 1904. It shared the fame with the falls. It was a modest building of wood and corrugated iron. There were only twelve single rooms and four doubles, a dining room and a bar. The first manager was Gavuzzi, an Italian. His chef was a Frenchman, the bar man from Chicago, and the waiters were Arabs.

When the hotel was first built, the railway line passed between it and the Victoria Falls Gorge. In 1908 a torrential storm dropped seven and one half inches of rain in four hours. The line was washed away.

By 1913 the tourists were pouring in. Five excursions by train came in a year from Capetown, South Africa. It was decided that the hotel would be rebuilt in brick. The work was started in 1912. By 1922, visitors had reached three thousand a year. The hotel was expanded. In 1946, the hotel was visited by King George VI, Queen Elizabeth, and the two Princesses, Elizabeth and Margaret. Princess Anne spent the night in 1983 in what is now known as the Livingston Suite. By 1947 the hotel accommodated some eleven thousand visitors. In 1992 the hotel was chosen as being one of the top fifty hotels in the world.

I believe that I was exhausted when I arrived at this historic hotel. There was a quick recovery when I had dinner with wine and music. I persuaded one of the waiters to dance with me.

Early in the morning we had a conducted tour of Victoria Falls. We walked four kilometers on a path skirting the falls. It was spectacular. There was a raft spinning around at the bottom of one of the gorges. This I caught on my movie camera. I spoke coaxingly to my Minolta, then captured several pictures of the falls—not the best photography. I had better luck filming back on the hotel grounds where there was a huge aged flamboyant tree covered with a profusion of vermillion blossoms.

Things were moving too fast. After this long walk, we were whisked off to a crocodile farm. There were mountains of crocodiles being bred and raised. Before I could catch my breath, it was time to catch a plane for Hwange National Park, Zimbabwe's largest.

We arrived at the Ivory Lodge at night. We went right out on a ride to a water hole. There were eighty-four elephants, zebras, cape buffalo, and giraffes. Wild dogs came in. We watched this scene for a long time, viewing the vestiges of a brilliant sunset.

Back at camp, steaks, baked potatoes, and a tossed salad were waiting for us. From the eating area, a trail led to my cabin. It was built up high in the trees. I had to climb stairs to get there. Little frogs on my bedside table kept me company through the night.

The next day we had a full day to explore the park. By this time, I was becoming satiated with all of the animal viewing and the astounding arenas of activity. Believe it or not, we had one more morning to live this dream world before we were transported to the Airport for Harare. After a few hours, we caught our flight to London. Soon we were on our way to Phoenix, Arizona where the scorpions, Gila monsters, tarantulas, centipedes, and rattlesnakes thrive. Wow, what a transition!

Barrancas del Cobre, Copper Canyon, Mexico
November 20, 1993

It would seem logical to bring to an end my fanciful opulent odyssey of ten years with my last trip to Africa in September, 1993. Ironically, this was not meant to be. In reality, I seemed to be prolonging the end.

It was a short, modest trip to Copper Canyon in Mexico that brings my story to an end. In November I flew from Phoenix to Los Mochis on the Sea of Cortez. This is a fertile agricultural area. Los Mochis means "place of turtles" in the Mayan Indian dialect. The place was established in 1903 by an American, Benjamin Johnson, who started a large sugar plantation and a sugar mill. Today, more than 750,000 acres are cultivated with crops of sugar cane, alfalfa, cotton, rice, and winter vegetables.

I was to take the famous train for Chihuahua. The Chihuahua Pacific railroad was inaugurated in November, 1961. It took ninety years from its conception to its completion. For centuries, thousands of square miles of fabulous mountains and canyons were only known to a few explorers, prospectors, and missionaries. It could only be reached by a difficult journey on burro or on foot.

The train took us on an ascent into the Sierra Madre Mountains on its way to Chihuahua. You travel from a little above sea level to almost 8000 feet in a little more than six hours. This railroad is considered to be one of the world's most fantastic engineering feats with its four miles of bridges spanning thirty-eight ravines. There are seventy or more tunnels piercing mountains along its route. It crosses a sprawling labyrinth of canyons. Until recently, it was the only land connection between Los Mochis and Chihuahua City.

The first night, I had little sleep in my room at the Hotel Colina, perched on a hill as its name suggests. The music of the happy Mexicans went on all night long. I had to get up at four o'clock to catch the six o'clock train.

In the beginning, we passed through flat low country called the Sinaloan Thornforest Life Zone. It is a cactus and thorntree jungle. As we proceeded, the scenery got more spectacular and rugged with many canyons and rivers. We continued our ascent toward Divisadero where I would get my first view of the Barrancas del Cobre. The train passed through El Fuerte. This was a fort established here in the late 16th century to protect settlers from rebellions. A few kilometers further, we passed over the Rio Fuerte on the longest bridge on the railroad. It is 1,637 feet long. Our next bridge spans the Rio Chinipas. That is the highest bridge on the railroad. It is 1000 feet in length and is three hundred and fifty five feet above the river. Next came a series of tunnels. There was literally one tunnel after another. At one point we had views of the tracks descending by curves and loops where three levels of the railroad were visible as well as tunnel number 49 and a twin waterfall.

I tried desperately to photograph, but the train was giving us a rough ride. I tried to hold steady and brace myself even in the precarious area between the cars. I was not very successful.

After about seven hours, we arrived in Divisadero. I did not stay in either of the two famous hotels perched on the canyon's rim. They appear to be clinging to the cliffs. They have a fantastic view of the rugged mountains and the precipitous chasm through which the Rio Urique runs. I was lodged in a small modest accommodation, the

Hotel Mansion Tarahumara. It was snuggled on a slope surrounded by trees. Nearby was a small pueblo. A miniature white church stood all alone with two bell towers on its roof, each embellished with a simple white cross. The hotel was built like a petite castle with a turret on each side of the main structure. The base of each one was ornate, one having a fringed-like enclosure circling it. Bright red cone-shaped caps adorned these turrets. All was painted white except for the red roof and cones.

The guests stayed in cabanas, separate from the main building. These cabins were absolutely charming. The walls were made of stone, assembled in a flagstone pattern. The furniture was rustic handmade. Between the red-curtained window and a huge wooden door, there hung a precious cosmetic stand with a large framed mirror. A small humble wooden chair stood in front of it. The door was made with a large semi-circle above with vertical pieces of lumber dropping to the floor. A panel of metal separated the semi-circle from the rest of the door.

In the main building, an open kitchen with a huge wood-burning stove was where I watched the jovial woman cook make homemade tortillas. The dining area was colorful with the same wooden furniture and bright red tablecloths. It was like being at home. There were not many visitors. The food was excellent.

A handsome young Mexican man, who played the guitar in the evening entertainment, acted as my guide. One afternoon, he, the cook, and I climbed up far behind the castle to the edge of the gorge. For two hours we watched the Tarahumara Indians, far below us, climbing around on the slopes where they live in caves. I zoomed in with my camera. They were like little colorful ants crawling about. Some of these same Indians gathered and sat in front of the hotel with their small adorable children. I have a picture of a mother weaving what appears to be fibers from a yucca plant. Her child is standing near her.

In the evening, after our long climb to the rim of the Barrancas, we had savory Sopa de elote and Chile rellenos for dinner. Afterwards, we gathered in front of the huge fireplace and listened to the guitars and singing.

One morning, Saul, my guide, took me in the van to the Hotel Posada Barrancas Mirador. It was terrifying to see this luxurious hotel clinging to the edge of the cliffs. I was so happy to be in my modest parador (inn), my castle. We continued on to a mercado (market) and to the tiny church. I entered and took pictures. It was divine. The exterior was so humble, but inside it was truly exquisite, so beautifully decorated. There was a small white altar, a Virgin Mary, flowers, a cross with Jesus on the left, and highly polished wooden ceiling and pews. So tiny, yet so majestic in its simplicity. I was overcome.

I spent the afternoon reading the Bible. The dinner fare was excellent—soup, T-bone steak, and string beans. We met at the fireplace on the balcony overlooking the dining room. There was a repeat musical performance.

I only spent a few nights here. I could have stayed a week. It was so charming. The nightly entertainment of guitars and singers was even attended one evening by the local priest. I didn't want to leave, but I had to catch the train again for Creel, an hour and a half farther towards Chihuahua.

The train was late. No one cared. It arrived at three and we were in Creel at four-thirty. In Creel, I was booked into the Parador de la Montana. It was more like a motel, but very comfortable. I rested and read the Bible. In the evening I had Sopa de elote (corn) again and broiled chicken a la parrilla.

Creel is the Tarahumara Indian capital of the Copper Canyon region. An incredible wilderness surrounds the area with immense canyons, forests, lakes, streams, and waterfalls. This is a lumber town of about five thousand people, nestled back in the mountains away from the edge of the canyon.

I signed up, along with a young newlywed couple, for a tour the first morning to the Clascada (waterfall) de Cusarare. I was not told that we had to walk for two hours. I awoke and pounded on their door, telling them that they must not miss this tour. The young couple seemed to be distracted or have other matters on their mind. I kept knocking on their door urging them to come with me on this delightful excursion. They finally appeared dressed for the occasion. We started off with the guide. After driving a short distance, we arrived at the trailhead. I had my doubts about the walk with my arthritis. It had come as a complete surprise to me. It turned out to be a fabulous hike. There were huge rock formations against the forested hills. We sat on these monstrous rocks with some Tarahumara Indians to be photographed. The young girl helped me over the rough spots and we arrived at the falls.

The falls were magnificent. I took so many pictures of my young friends who were so desperately in love, with the falls as a backdrop. They, being more agile than I, hiked down to a ledge at the base of the falls. They were kissing. I zoomed in. Then they hiked up to a ledge near the top of the falls where they embraced. I had a nice series of photos to send to them after I returned home.

It was time to catch the train again bound for Chihuahua. I purchased a burrito from a vendor at the small station in La Junta, which was about the halfway mark of our journey. Between Creel and La Junta, we went through a mountainous environment with beautiful valleys, each with its picturesque minuscule village. We arrived in Chihuahua at nine in the evening. By the time I got into the hotel, I was tired and starved. I grabbed a bite in the hotel restaurant just to survive. I would not recommend it to anyone.

On Thanksgiving Day, I had a tasty breakfast, then walked to the main plaza to photograph the Cathedral. I walked, and took buses, and taxis trying to find a Thanksgiving dinner of cabrito (goat). I had to give up.

When I talk about the Barrancas del Cobre, not many people have any idea of what I am talking about. I urge everyone to investigate this adventure. It was most unusual. The engineering of this railroad and the views it provided were breathtaking. The hidden villages, the waterfalls, and the canyons were like a fantasy. The Tarahumara Indians, dressed in their bright native clothes, appeared everywhere out of the forest and from among the boulders. This was pure enchantment.

I am at the end of my sojourn as well as the end of my odyssey. Sometimes I question the drama and the uniqueness of my final trip. It was not so eventful as my other excursions. Perhaps this was the best way to end a fabulous ten years, close to home and in an arena not explored by many.

This was to be a ten-year account of my traveling about, so I must be true to my promise. Now, if I can come up with an appropriate way to terminate this chronicle, you may relax, weary reader.

A brief epilogue may be called for. Since 1993, I continued to pursue and satisfy my lust for travel. There were trips to Ireland, Tahiti, New Zealand, and Puerto Rico. A snorkeling trip to Tulum, near Cancun, Mexico, completely captivated me for a week. A 4-wheel excursion in the red rocks of Sedona, Arizona and hiking in the Chiricahua National Monument mountains, the Cochise Apache stronghold in southeastern Arizona, were meshed in between the longer trips.

I am tempted to continue with a detailed sequel, but I shall not do so. This is really the end.